NATIVE TREES *&* FORESTS OF IRELAND

NATIVE TREES & FORESTS OF IRELAND

David Hickie / Photography Mike O'Toole

Gill & Macmillan

Gill & Macmillan Ltd
Hume Avenue
Park West, Dublin 12
with associated companies
throughout the world
www.gillmacmillan.ie

© Text: David Hickie 2002
© Photography: Mike O'Toole 2002
© Illustrations: Austin Carey 2002

0 7171 3411 3

Index compiled by Cover To Cover
Design and print origination:
Brenda Dermody
Colour reproduction by Typeform Repro, Dublin
Printed by ColourBooks Ltd, Dublin

This book is typeset in Sabon 9.5 on 12.5

A CIP catalogue record for this book is
available from the British Library.

5 4 3 2 1

This book is dedicated to
the late Freda Rountree

CONTENTS

Foreword

An intuitive sense of our place in nature, of the
interactive wholeness of the Earth, is confirmed
every day through science. On this small island,
with its harsh history of wear-and-tear, there is
a growing liberation of the ordinary human
feeling for trees and the networks of life – the
ecosystems – they support.

The ocean hillside where I live has the typical bleak beauty of the West. Clumps of wind-shaped sycamores and conifers crouched around the farmhouses seem only to dramatise the lack of shelter. But tucked away in rocky folds are shreds and remnants of woods that were never planted: they grew up and hung on naturally at the edges of human activity. Behind the *creggans* or rocky crags at the shore are ferny grottoes of oaks, hollies and hazel; in a ravine at the foot of the mountain, the oaks lean out over waterfalls and are joined by aspens that shiver in the wind.

In this rugged setting, our native woodland has been pushed to its last, remote refuges, just beyond the reach of browsing cattle and sheep. All over Ireland, there are patches of woods with this ragged, left-over look, as if we grudged them a living. Their very survival often seems to be by chance. Yet, even as a background, the trees persist in being beautiful at every season, their branches and birdsong an indelible part of our sense of place, our quality of life. As this book describes and celebrates, the spirit of the woods is at last being revived for and by the nation.

A general re-awakening to nature in Ireland is part of a wider global recognition of the human harm done to the planet. An intuitive sense of our place in nature, of the interactive wholeness of the Earth, is confirmed every day through science. On this small island, with its harsh history of wear-and-tear, there is a growing liberation of the ordinary human feeling for trees and the networks of life – the ecosystems – they support.

As David Hickie shows us, a woodland of mingled native trees is one of the richest ecosystems anywhere. The trees that are native to Ireland have been with us for anything up to 10,000 years, since the last Ice Age, and our birds and insects are specially adapted to them for food and shelter. The more ancient the wood, the more diverse and intricate their plant and animal life has become.

Just north of where I live, beyond Croagh Patrick, is Brackloon Wood, once part of an old estate. At its heart are stands of lofty oaks that grew up almost two centuries ago from the stumps and seedlings of their ancient predecessors. They form a typical 'Atlantic' oakwood, its branches fringed with ferns and lichens. Now, indeed, the trees and their passengers breathe the moist air even more freely, for conifers planted 50 years ago are being cleared by Coillte with Forest Service funding and their ground planted with a new generation of oaks grown from the wood's own acorns. They will grow up together with seedlings of the wood's other native trees: ash, birch, wild cherry, rowan.

Just one tall oak at Brackloon has more than 50 kinds of lichen growing on it, from mossy base to the tips of its topmost twigs. In one square metre of brown earth beneath it are some 260 earthworms. Beetles, bats, badgers, birds are all woven into a teeming web of life that takes even dead and fallen trees into its cycle of renewal. Studied from year to year, the lessons learned from changes in its ecosystem will help in restoring the People's Millennium Forests scattered across the island.

Oaks have come to symbolise our lost native woodlands, but they are only one of our native trees: even the modest willow is quite as important to the whole range of insect life. The value and beauty of diversity shine out of the pages that follow. Yews have their own wild character and long history on the island; the pines now called 'Scots' were just as Irish until their mysterious extinction as a native species. Given the trials now under way on the slopes of Killarney National Park, it is not an impossible dream that *Pinus sylvestris*, so graceful and individual a conifer, will one day cloak great tracts of overgrazed uplands and cut-over midlands in an open and airy forest, home to red squirrels and pine martens.

Meanwhile, the new Forest Service Native Woodland Scheme is an exciting opportunity – in some cases, a last chance – to rescue, replenish and extend the surviving fragments of semi-natural woodland. For many, the priorities must be to fence out the livestock that chew up every regenerating seedling, to clear the rhododendron and laurel that choke the woodland floor, and perhaps to coppice trees here and there in order to let in some light.

In Ireland, as elsewhere, the whole long cycle of growth and rebirth in our native trees has been lost to common experience. People tend to think of trees in human terms, as if they had fixed life-spans and were doomed by hollow trunks or dead boughs – both entirely natural in a tree's leisurely old age. Clear-felling of commercial conifer plantations has fixed a 'time to die' image in our minds, along with the impression that woods, once cut down, are destroyed.

In fact, most of our native trees have immense powers of renewal, growing again from the stump or the roots, or from the trunk cut well above the ground. In simple techniques of woodsmanship – coppicing and pollarding – our forebears took regular crops of poles and fuelwood, almost indefinitely. Great 'stools' of coppiced trees, sometimes several metres across, are a sure mark of an ancient wood, no less than the wood anemones, bluebells and wild garlic that speak of the passage of centuries.

In the oldest and least disturbed of the woods, precious reservoirs of tree-seed and plant species, the main aim will, indeed, be protection and restoration of biodiversity. In more damaged settings, and the creation of new native woodlands or extensions, a revival of close-to-nature silviculture seems to point the way forward. Selective felling and coppicing for high-value, craft-based uses of timber can still give us woods with continuous cover and a naturally healthy ecosystem to serve as wildlife refuges and corridors through the landscape.

The long struggle for awareness of our native woodland has often seemed to fall upon a few dogged pioneers. But, with the turn of the Millennium, a will to act has risen like sap in springtime birches, not least in the state-sponsored schemes described herein. David Hickie has no illusions about the wider imbalance between the national targets for conifer planting and those for native broadleaf trees. He tells of popular battles to protect ancient trees and woods under threat, some fought by local communities, others by idealists and activists resisting every fresh whine of a chainsaw.

Many people who admire our native trees see their first value in human delight or profit. Others, like the 'deep ecologists', show a fierce regard for wild forest for its own sake, the bigger and less disturbed the better. In the words and pictures that follow, there is inspiration for everyone.

Michael Viney *March 2002*

This book was conceived as a celebration of the People's Millennium Forests Project. The idea of marking the new Millennium by restoring our native woodland resource began back in 1997 when a group of people met in Kilkenny to put together a restoration project that would be both imaginative and far-seeing. The driving force was the late Freda Rountree, then Chairperson of the Heritage Council. The Woodlands of Ireland group was formed with funding from Dúchas The Heritage Service, from the Forest Service of the Department of the Marine and Natural Resources, and from the Heritage Council. The group brought together all statutory and voluntary organisations concerned with the restoration and enhancement of our native woodland resource. They sought financial aid for a Millennium project involving native woodland restoration. Funding amounting to 5.08 million euro was provided by the following: AIB, 2.54 million euro; the National Millennium Committee, 2.03 million euro; and the Forest Service of the Department of the Marine and Natural Resources, 0.51 million euro.

Coillte was designated the task of managing the project and work began in 1999 on planting 1.2 million trees – one for every household – and on the other aspects of the project that are outlined in this book.

Native Trees & Forests of Ireland came together through the work of a very dedicated team: David Hickie provided the text, and he has a wonderful feel for native woodlands, while Michael Viney's foreword puts native woodlands in context. The book is enhanced by Mike O'Toole's wonderful photographs and by Brenda Dermody's design. Peigín Doyle helped with editing. Moving the project along gently were Breda Keena and Eveleen Coyle. To everybody involved in the project a very special thanks.

John McLoughlin
Project Manager
People's Millennium Forests Project

PEOPLE'S MILLENNIUM FORESTS

1   Ballygannon, Rathdrum, County Wicklow
2   Camolin, County Wexford
3   Castle Archdale, County Fermanagh
4   Coill an Fhaltaigh, County Kilkenny
5   Cullentra, County Sligo
6   Derrygill, County Galway
7   Derrygorry, County Monaghan
8   Favour Royal, County Tyrone
9   Glengarra, County Tipperary
10 Lacca, County Laois
11 Muckross (Killarney National Park),
    County Kerry
12 Portlick, County Westmeath
13 Rossacroo-na-Loo, County Kerry
14 Rosstura, County Galway
15 Shelton, County Wicklow
16 Tourmakeady, County Mayo

*Based on Ordnance Survey Ireland by
permission of the Government Permit No. 7547
© Ordnance Survey Ireland and Government
of Ireland*

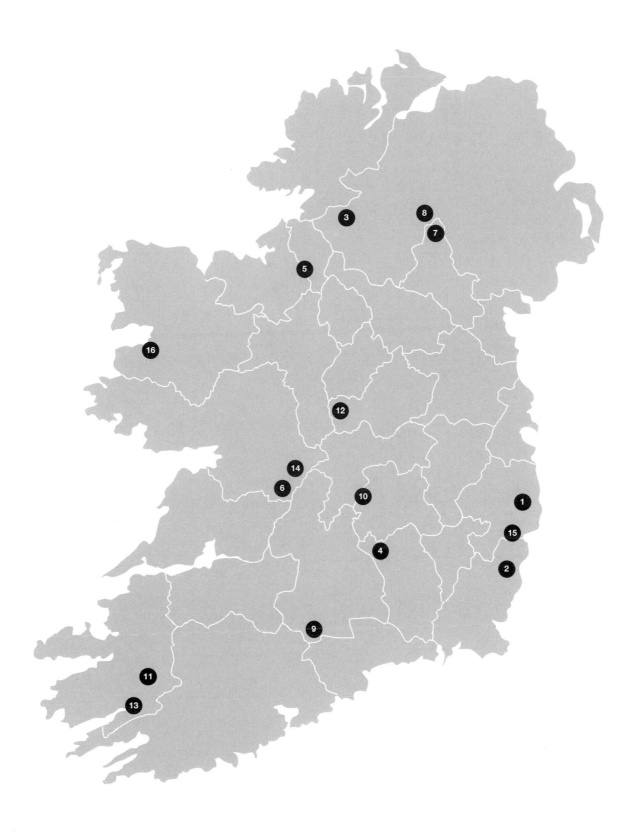

1 The Ancient Wildwood

This is the story of how the great forests and native trees arrived in Ireland; how they were pushed back and cut down over centuries; and how, at the end of the twentieth century, the tide of loss was first turned and the dream of creating a new – or recreating an older – landscape took root again.

It has taken nearly 9,000 years of human occupation to give Ireland the landscape that we know today. Green fields; hedgerows dotted with occasional large sycamore, holly or ash; distant, rounded hills planted with dark green forests or grazed by flocks of sheep – these images are so familiar we would be forgiven for thinking that it was always like this and that landscape never changes.

But nothing stands still. The grassy, open countryside so characteristic of Ireland today has only looked like this for a comparatively short time, measured by nature's clock.

Before the first settlers arrived, Ireland looked completely different. A deep layer of ice had covered the land for thousands of years. This was followed by a thick blanket of forest, and it was a heavily wooded terrain that our ancestors encountered when they arrived about 9,000 years ago. Many changes followed on from generations of human habitation and by the nineteenth century a new landscape had emerged – bare, grassy, almost treeless.

At the beginning of the twentieth century only one per cent of the total land area was under trees. Now, at the beginning of a new millennium, a move is afoot to undo the damage of centuries and bring back something that was nearly lost – our native trees and woodlands.

This is the story of how the great forests and native trees arrived in Ireland; how they were pushed back and cut down over centuries; and how, at the end of the twentieth century, the tide of loss was first turned and the dream of creating a new – or recreating an older – landscape took root again.

Opposite: A deforested landscape in Connemara. Thousands of years ago, these hills were covered in native forest.

HOW THE WOODLANDS DEVELOPED

Over 12,000 years ago, a bird flying over the Irish countryside would have seen a bare, almost totally white landscape, similar to Greenland or the polar ice caps. A huge sheet of ice, several miles deep, covered the land. A few southern areas may have remained free of ice and snow for short and fickle summers.

Ireland, at that time, was not even an island. The sea level had fallen dramatically during the Ice Age – to about 120 metres below today's level. Ireland was joined to Britain and both land-masses were a peninsula of continental Europe, connected by the great ice sheet. It had been this way for over 100,000 years.

Then, about 10,000 ago, the Ice Age came to an end. Gradually the climate had warmed and the glaciers relaxed their icy grip. The forests and grasslands marched northwards again, and the forest animals and plants travelled with them.

As the ice melted, the sea level rose over a period of just a few thousand years. There was only a relatively short time for plants and animals to reach Ireland, over the newly-exposed land-bridge, before the rising sea cut off the country from Britain and the continental mainland, and Ireland became an island. Many species never reached here in time. It was this accident of climate that left us with the comparatively small number of native tree and wildlife species we have inherited. It explains why Britain and continental Europe have a greater variety of native wild animals, plants and trees than is found here.

After the ice cap melted, Ireland became, first, a country of tundra and, then, of grasslands. The pollen record suggests that the first tree to reach the island when the climate warmed was the juniper, a shrubby

4

conifer. This was followed by willow and then by birch. Over 500 years, these three tough pioneers colonised the rich meadows. Hazel followed birch 250 years later and was followed, in turn, by pine, which took about 1,000 years to reach Donegal from the south-west. Finally, about 8500 BC the great forest trees of oak and elm began to dominate the wildwood on the better soils. This phase of woodland development lasted until about 7000 BC, when the wildwood had reached its peak.

So, 9,000 years ago, there was a country covered in forests of oak and elm, with other trees growing beneath the canopy of the great trees, and all teeming with animal and bird life.

However, by the nineteenth and early twentieth centuries, Ireland was a bare, grassy, almost treeless country. The only woods that existed were tiny, scattered remnants of older forests, or planted woodlands, many on old landed estates.

What happened to the great forests over those 9,000 years? The answer is – people.

The woodlands were flourishing when the first people arrived in Ireland. As they pulled their boats up out of the tide or tentatively crossed one of the remaining land-bridges between Ireland and Britain, and scanned the horizon, there would have been nothing to see but unbroken stretches of forest, swamps and occasional bog, interrupted only by rivers, lakes and hills.

The first visitors to these shores used flint and other stone implements. Farming had not yet been adopted and these people were hunters and gatherers who relied on the bounty of the land and tended to move around seasonally, perhaps following their prey. Archaeologists studying their early settlements have found the remains of wild pig, duck, pigeon and grouse bones, as well

as a variety of fish and shellfish. This gives an indication of the reliance of these Mesolithic peoples on fishing and hunting game. They also gathered nuts and berries, and may have stored hazelnuts for the winter. Most likely they followed the rivers upstream, looking for suitable places to settle. It would have been a daunting prospect. In their first ventures into the forest, they would have seen massive, ancient trees towering above them. The trunks of dead trees would have lain on the forest floor like shipwrecked hulks. Progress would have been slow because there would have been no paths, and scrub and briars would have barred their way.

The swampy areas would have been even more difficult to cross, until the newcomers reached a lake or river, where huge flocks of waterfowl would have taken flight at their approach. At night, around the fire, they might have heard wolves howling at the moon, or the sound of grunting and twigs snapping as a family of wild boar passed by. By day, they might have seen bears feeding along the riverbanks before disappearing into the forest.

We can imagine the type of woodland the first settlers saw when they were hunting and fishing. The areas that are good farmland today, like Cork and Limerick, were cloaked with elm, oak and alder, while the less fertile hills in Mayo, Galway, Kerry and Donegal were carpeted in pine and birch. One could get some idea of what the Midlands might have looked like by visiting the great broadleaf forest of Bialowieza on the Polish/Russian border, which is the closest that Europe can provide to natural broadleaf forest. The ancient Caledonian pine forest in the central Highlands of Scotland, which has

Opposite: Mosses forming a luxuriant carpet on the fissured bark of an old oak tree

been growing continuously from primeval times, gives us some idea of what our own hills were like when they were still naturally forested.

This scenario is almost unthinkable for us today, because we are so accustomed to surveying the treeless expanses of this grassy island. But it was a reality for the people who were adventurous enough to reach here and for their descendants over the generations.

Our first settlers probably followed a relatively unchanged lifestyle for several thousand years, although there were some changes over time in the nature of the stonework that they produced. They may well have lived in the same timeless way that the aboriginal peoples in Australia or Africa still do today. They would have held the trees, mountains and other parts of the landscape in reverence, not just because the land ensured food, warmth and survival but also because such places had a religious significance, as abodes of the gods or as sources of wisdom and knowledge. Shadowy echoes of such beliefs survive even today in folklore and folk customs (described in Chapter 3). Such lore may have helped some woodland places or individual trees to survive the pressure of development over the centuries.

The timeless way of life of our aboriginal peoples was gradually brought to an end when a new type of activity began around 5,700 years ago, probably associated with an influx of people to Ireland. The new activity was agriculture, associated with a sedentary lifestyle, and the changes that began at this time were among the most significant ever to occur on this island. It was at this time that the transformation of Ireland from thick forest to open landscape began. The first forest clearances may have resembled those of the European settlers in North America from the 1500s onwards. And these people must have displaced the aboriginal hunter-gatherers in the process, just as European colonists to the New World displaced the native North Americans. They brought with them their cattle and sheep – excavations at Mount Sandel suggest that there were already wild pigs in Ireland. They may even have imported red deer: the earliest evidence of red deer so far discovered dates from 4300 BC.

These late Stone Age, or Neolithic, farmers were very resourceful. After all, it was they who built the great passage tombs of Newgrange, Knowth and Dowth. They brought with them farming and building techniques that had fanned out from the Mediterranean, and they must have built boats similar to currachs to bring people and animals across the sea.

They introduced to Ireland the greatest ecological experiment the world has ever known – agriculture. Woodland had to be cleared for farming and so, over the centuries, the wildwoods yielded inexorably to more open country. But it was not quite the wholesale clearance one might imagine. Small plots were made where crops were grown and livestock grazed. When the soil became exhausted, the farmers moved on to another plot, and so on. The abandoned plots were then invaded by hazel and later by forest trees. The roots of the trees could bring up more nutrients from deep within the soil, making it fertile once more, and the farmers could return to the places they had left decades earlier. This technique of 'forest fallow' has been practised in other countries and on other continents.

Additional factors such as climate and disease helped to weaken the grip of the forests. Around 5,100 years ago, there was a

Opposite: *In a typical oak/birch woodland*

dramatic decline in elm, resulting possibly from an epidemic such as Dutch elm disease. This phenomenon may have contributed to the efforts of our early pioneers to clear the woodlands. Studies of the pollen record reveal that from the very first woodland clearances right through to the Middle Ages, hazel scrub was a striking characteristic of the landscape – and quite possibly the wildwood never fully recovered from this overlay.

Still, the forest had not shrunk to any great extent until, perhaps, around the first century AD when our main conifer, Scots pine, probably died out, a victim of woodland clearances and the change to a cooler, wetter climate.

This climate change also helped to bring about the emergence of bogs. In the Midlands, where modern-day, giant Bord na Móna machines have scraped away the peat, the skeletons of Ireland's former forests have been exhumed: thousands of fossil tree stumps stand in piles by the roadsides, waiting to be burned or fashioned into strange, exotic shapes by woodturners and sculptors. And in the eroding hills of Mayo and Sligo, the stumps of pines that had been smothered by a protective covering of blanket bog can be seen, their stumps still bearing the scars of pre-bog fire and axe.

In the Céide Fields of north Mayo, ancient fields, walls and settlements were buried beneath the peat, as if nature had wanted to move on by pulling a tarpaulin over an entire way of life. Where the great woods once stood, now the boglands, in their austere beauty, stretch out over the horizon.

We have seen how the first forest clearances began; how the elm declined and the Scots pine was lost; how the climate cooled and the creeping bog blanketed much of the area

Opposite: Arbutus or strawberry tree

covered by the forests. But the greatest force to press on the woodlands and push them into decline was the human population. As numbers grew, there was increasing pressure on woodland resources to sustain life. The very usefulness of trees was the cause of the decline. The stories, recounted in Chapter 2, of how some well-known forests and woodlands fared over the centuries, are examples of how the great forests throughout the country were exploited and destroyed.

But this is a story with a future, as well as a present and a past. The woodlands do survive in both the northern and southern parts of the country. Now, at the start of the Third Millennium, the efforts of pioneering campaigners have created greater awareness of the beauty and ecological value of broadleaf forests. The native woodlands contain predominantly trees of native origin and they are important because they symbolise for us today how the country looked before human beings arrived. Actions like the People's Millennium Forests Project in the Republic, in which 16 ancient woodlands are being protected and replanted, and the decision in Northern Ireland to restore to native woodland many sites that currently carry plantations, are ensuring that native forests will live and grow long into the future.

2 Native Woods around the Country

The bleakest times for Ireland's woods were the nineteenth and early twentieth centuries. In the early 1800s, Ireland's population was expanding, and there was a continuous demand for more farmland to provide food. The break-up of the old estates in the late 1800s triggered a further wave of felling as timber merchants scoured the last woods for good timber. Photographs from the turn of the twentieth century show an almost treeless landscape. Only a remnant survived, but today this remnant is the jewel in nature's crown in Ireland.

It is difficult for us to appreciate just how important timber was to the world before the Industrial Revolution. Timber was to Elizabethan England as oil is to our economy today – an essential source of energy and raw material for economic development. The great European sea powers depended upon a continuous supply of high-quality timber for their great wooden ships, not only for carrying goods and people but also for their navies. For England especially, being an island, sea power was inseparable from timber supply, and the Admiralty kept a keen eye on the forests as well as the coastline. Since Ireland had been effectively colonised by that time, it too was seen as a valuable source of timber, and worth fighting for.

Wood was also consumed in vast quantities for smelting ore, as firewood, to make staves for barrels, and for building. Such was the level of demand that, by the end of the eighteenth century, Ireland had virtually run out of timber, and had to import increasing quantities. This may be one of the reasons why Dublin Corporation ordered that houses in the city had to be built out of brick and stone rather than timber.

How could an entire country just run out of timber? Presumably because successive governments and the ruling classes were not sufficiently organised or far-sighted to manage the remaining native woods or plant enough trees for the future, although exotic species had been planted on some landed estates since the sixteenth century. However, for a period during the eighteenth and nineteenth centuries, the Royal Dublin Society (RDS) provided a planting grant scheme in recognition of the fact that our woodland resources were dying off. Charleville Wood, described later in this chapter, benefited from such a scheme.

Clearance for agriculture was another major cause of deforestation. Beginning in the Late Stone Age, it continued right through to the present day. Even up to the end of the 1970s, landowners were clearing patches of woodland for agricultural improvement, with the aid of state funding.

The bleakest times for Ireland's woods were the nineteenth and early twentieth centuries. In the early 1800s, Ireland's population was expanding, and there was a continuous demand for more farmland to provide food. The break-up of the old estates in the late 1800s triggered a further wave of felling as timber merchants scoured the last woods for good timber. Photographs from the turn of the twentieth century show an almost treeless landscape. Only a remnant survived, but today this remnant is the jewel in nature's crown in Ireland.

In this chapter, we make a lightning tour of some well-known native woods around the country. The story of these woods epitomises the history of forestry in Ireland. If mistakes and neglect occurred in the past, it is a journey that finishes with a message of hope and renewal.

TOMNAFINNOGUE WOOD

Set amid the fertile, rolling countryside of south-west Wicklow is Tomnafinnogue Wood, the last remnant of the once-great woodland of Shillelagh. Since earliest times, the area was noted for its oak forests and for the famous Shillelagh stick. Tradition has it that the oak forests supplied the celebrated beams in Westminster Hall during the reign of William 1 of England, around 1087-1100.

During the period of intense destruction of the native woods from the 1600s onwards, a

Previous: Colonisation of a native wood in Killarney by sycamore (a non-native species) Opposite: A woodland walk in Tomnafinnogue Wood, County Wicklow

tradition of careful management of the wood-lands at Shillelagh is recorded, something which was then unusual. The woods were part of the Coolattin estate, which was owned by the Earl Fitzwilliam. However, the presence of foresters throughout the centuries did not prevent the woods being gradually reduced to approximately 60 hectares by the early 1990s. Names such as Brow Wood, Quail's Wood and Shuttle's Wood are now merely memories, but some of the felled areas have been replanted. In time, they will become mature native woods once more.

A walk through this once proud woodland is likely to be quiet and solitary. Few people know where it is, and fewer still visit it. A hop over a gate and a walk along a path bring you to an ancient stone bridge encrusted with vegetation, spanning the Shillelagh River. Then a path brings you alongside the clean, lazily flowing little river and through the wood. If you veer off the path towards the water, you can see signs of otters along the sandy banks and evidence of deer coming down to drink at dawn and dusk. The shrill whistle of a startled Sika deer confirms the evidence.

The oaks are mainly of fairly good quality, growing in deep, fertile soil. Many are tall and straight, unlike the gnarled and weathered specimens of the West. The smaller trees growing underneath the main forest canopy, called the understorey, are mostly holly and hazel. A few non-native trees, including some magnificent old beeches, still survive. In spring, there are carpets of bluebells and in autumn, the *fraochán* or blueberries ripen. The little path ends where some wet woodland of willow and alder begins, and the wood ends abruptly with farmland on the other side of the fence.

Today, the wood is strictly protected as a Special Area of Conservation and it will, in time, become a nature reserve.

Tomnafinnogue was originally bought for the people by Wicklow County Council but it is now owned by Dúchas The Heritage Service. That Tomnafinnogue survives at all is due to the efforts of some dedicated people who campaigned for years to save the wood (see Chapter 7). Although it is a native woodland site, it could well have been planted after the original wood was felled. It is recorded that the woodland was included in a replanting programme in the late eighteenth century. Strictly speaking, therefore, it is probably not as natural as some other native woods. But it does show how well native oaks will grow, given the chance.

GLENDALOUGH

Glendalough is a sheltered, comfortably wooded place. On one side of the Upper Lake, the branches of old oaks stretch down to the lake surface with its clean, gravelly bottom while, on the other, the orange-brown bracken mixes with the bottle-green of old Scots pines. Looking up the famous valley, the woodland peters out and yields to the bleak moorland beyond. But from the Upper Lake down past the village of Laragh towards Rathdrum is a strip of native woodland that clothes the valley sides.

It is hard to imagine that, by the early nineteenth century, Glendalough had been stripped of trees. The forest was literally mined, as coal and oil are today, for firewood and charcoal. In his *Reading the Irish Landscape*, Frank Mitchell contrasts a drawing of Glendalough as it used to be with a present-day photograph. The starkness of the landscape just a few centuries ago reminds one of Donegal, not Wicklow.

Opposite & overleaf: Tomnafinnogue Wood, a remnant of the once-great Shillelagh woodlands

Charcoal (meaning 'charred coal') was made with kindling. Lengths of timber were stacked around a central post. Once the pile reached about head height, bracken and sods of earth were placed on top. The central post was then removed and some burning charcoal was dropped into the hole. A grass sod was placed over the hole to control the air supply and thus ensure that the wood was charred and not burned.

The once-bare valley of Glendalough is a symbol of the treelessness that characterised Ireland for so long. The deforested nature of the country in the nineteenth century led the writer Thomas Carlyle in 1850 to describe Ireland as 'one of the barest, raggedest countries now known; far too ragged a country, with patches of beautiful park and fine cultivation, like shreds of bright scarlet on a beggar's clouted coat'.

Outside the walled and wooded estates was a poor, landless rural population struggling to make ends meet. And of course, when Carlyle wrote, hundreds of thousands had already died in the Famine. It is not surprising that the wooded estates became associated with privilege and the denial of even basic rights to the majority, leaving a folk memory that was to hinder the case for conservation in the twentieth century.

The oaks grew again in Glendalough, not because of any conscious management but because demand for wood collapsed when coal, and later oil, were found to be better substitutes. In the late twentieth century, the threat was not of wholesale clearance but of re-planting with conifers. Today, the remnant broadleaf woods are strictly protected in the Glendalough and Vale of Clara Nature Reserves. Glendalough, in turn, forms the centrepiece of the Wicklow Mountains National Park. A two-metre high fence protects the young trees from browsing by the numerous deer, and the conifers that remain will be removed as they grow towards maturity. Its future is assured. But one wonders if many visitors to this beautiful area realise how naked were the steep valley sides overlooking the ancient monastic city only two centuries ago.

CHARLEVILLE WOOD

Some say the famous King Oak in Charleville Wood in Offaly is 400 years old; others claim that it could be even 800 years old and that it was growing before the Charleville estate was first established. It even survived a lightning strike 40 years ago.

The woods at Charleville are now regarded as among the most important of their type (ash, oak and hazel) in Ireland and Europe. They hold a rich diversity of wildlife as well as giving a home to magnificent old oaks. Historical records of the wood reach back to the early 1600s when a formal grant of the lands of Tullamore was made to Sir John Moore under the plantation of James I. In the 1700s, the Bury family owned it, and the current owner is David Hutton Bury.

An account of Charleville demesne in 1812 states that: 'it contains nearly 1,500 statute acres, most delightfully wooded with fine full-grown timber, and a considerable part is planted with young trees, for which Lord Charleville has received the Dublin Society's premium; these plantations are carefully fenced from cattle, and in the utmost possible heart and vigour. A large trace of bog, which has been drained, is now preparing for another extensive plantation without-side the demesne to the bounds of the estate, and the trees are to be had from the nurseries within.

Opposite: Woodland floor carpeted with leaves of native oak and ash
Overleaf: A carpet of bluebells on the woodland floor at Glendalough

The undulating hills so peculiar to this country have the most pleasing effect, and when planted are truly picturesque and engaging.'

The 'Dublin Society's premium' was Ireland's first forestry grant scheme. It was made by the Royal Dublin Society (now in Ballsbridge) to encourage landowners to reverse the devastation of the previous few centuries.

In an ironic twist of fate, even though Charleville managed to survive the ravages of the eighteenth and nineteenth centuries, a new by-pass through the wood was threatened as recently as 2000. Fortunately, this will not happen now.

THE GEARAGH

Today, all over Europe, forests alongside rivers are very rare. They were the first to be targeted in man's onward march across the land. They occupied the fertile lowlands and competed for space with housing and agriculture, and later, in the twentieth century, with dams. If they were not destroyed by drainage, they were flooded.

This is why The Gearagh is one of the most interesting and important forests in Ireland, and is an outstanding example of such woodland, even by European standards. It is the best Irish example of an alluvial forest – a forest growing in the flood plain of a river.

The name The Gearagh is a literal translation from the Irish, *An Gaoire*, meaning 'Wooded River'. It lies on the River Lee near Macroom in County Cork. It was not totally untouched by development: in the 1950s, about half the area was acquired for an Electricity Supply Board hydro-electric scheme. What remains is a site of high ecological value, being an ancient forest on a broad, braided river channel on the flood plain of the Lee.

The usual oaks dominate here, together with ash, birch, hazel, willow and alder. The unpolluted streams and wooded islets are an important habitat for wildfowl and in the grasslands there is some rare flora.

It is unlikely that there has been any recent interference with the woods, and so one can use them to imagine what many lowland river valleys must have looked like thousands of years ago, before the bogs developed. As the population expanded, grazing and burning would have damaged the woods and then, in more recent times, the rivers would have been gradually tamed by drainage schemes and hemmed in to prevent their flood waters spilling over onto farmland and settlements.

KILLARNEY

The road west past The Gearagh leads to Killarney, the home of Ireland's most celebrated and extensive native woods. Looking down the Killarney valley from Ladies' View there is a special panorama untypical of the rest of Ireland: broadleaf woodland clothes the slopes and climbs up the mountains, eventually petering out into expansive moorland. This is Killarney National Park, famed throughout the world for its wonderful scenery and its woodland and lakes.

The moist, mild Atlantic climate favours the growth of a lush flora which drapes the trees. Ferns and mosses cling like green fleeces to the trunks in this damp, rainforest-like environment. Oak, again, is the predominant type of tree in Killarney, but there are also several less common species. The first is the strawberry tree. The south-west of Ireland is the only area in Britain or Ireland where it is a native; its next closest station is northern Spain. The second notable tree is the yew, a

Opposite: The old stump of an oak tree

native conifer known by most of us from churchyards. Here, in Killarney's Reenadinna Wood on the Muckross peninsula, it grows wild in Ireland's only native yew wood.

Killarney has an unlikely history and new aspects have been added recently. The authors of *Killarney National Park: A Place to Treasure*, discovered that the woods, which were thought to have existed from primeval times, had been drastically interfered with by people from 4,000 years ago onwards. Like Glendalough, mining was practised here from antiquity – there was copper in Killarney, lead and silver in Glendalough – so the trees were used for smelting ore. Bronze Age farmers also exerted a huge influence, and the variety of trees that characterised the ancient forest gradually changed to the oak that has been so dominant during recorded history.

Arthur Young, an eighteenth-century travel writer, remarked in 1780 that Derrycunnihy Wood was 'part cut down, much of it mangled, and the rest inhabited by coopers, boat-builders, carpenters and turners'. Walking through the wood today on the road to Kenmare, one could imagine that it was primeval. In fact, it is not that old, but it is probably in the best condition of all of Killarney's oak woods.

Killarney's woods posed a mystery to scientists. They asked why, if the woods were ancient, there were no really old trees. The answer could be that heavy grazing, which was practised from Elizabethan times, declined drastically during or after the Famine, when the livestock were eaten. This would have allowed the trees that had germinated to survive past their vulnerable early years. Also, many of the existing trees that had survived from Tudor times were

felled for firewood and timber or had died of old age by the end of the 1800s. This left the generation of relatively young oaks we see now.

The history of Killarney's woods shows us that, even if there is only a part of the ecosystem left, woodland will regenerate quite easily if the conditions are right. The story does not end there. Our new relationship with native woods may yet result in the woods expanding further – not just the Killarney woods but many others too. This will be considered in Chapter 7.

Opposite: A rich growth of lichens on a birch tree, indicating an unpolluted atmosphere.

3 Myth, Magic and Spirit

For many of us, there is an unspoken
reverence for nature's mystique, which is
waiting for some catalyst, some turning point,
to allow it to express itself. All over Ireland,
people are becoming more conscious of their
surroundings and their relationship with the
natural world. Because of the contribution
they make to our sense of place, our heritage
and our imagination, native woods are
attracting the greatest interest of all.

In May 1999, *The Irish Times* reported that a Mr Eddie Lenihan, one of Ireland's best-known folklorists and storytellers, had delivered a stern warning to Clare County Council about the destruction of a hawthorn bush. He claimed that if the fairy thorn at Latoon outside Newmarket-on-Fergus was bulldozed to make way for a by-pass, it could result in misfortune and possibly death for those who would use the new road. According to Mr Lenihan, the site of the fairy bush 'is sacred ground; it doesn't revert to being a normal place'. Perhaps mindful of the dire warnings, the county engineer, after surveying the fairy thorn bush in the plans, confirmed that the council had found that it would now be able to incorporate the lone hawthorn into the proposed by-pass.

Another story is told by Ben Simon, a forester with the Forest of Belfast, of how a hawthorn bush was linked with the collapse of the ill-fated De Lorean car factory at Dunmurry. A local resident remembers her mother saying that, as a child, she used to hear the maids talking about the 'wee folk'. Mill girls who crossed the area on their way to work in the morning would say they had seen signs of the 'wee folk' by the tree. When bulldozers were clearing the land before the factory was built, the ground around the hawthorn was left untouched. The workmen even refused a direct order from the American site manager to cut it down and ignored an inducement of $100 buried under the tree. But one day the tree was gone and, from that day, the car plant was said to be ill-founded or perhaps even cursed. The factory closed soon afterwards.

These are just two of the many tales in Irish tree folklore that reach back into ancient

Previous & opposite: Rag trees, a carry-over from our pagan past

times, when certain trees were believed to have magical properties and powers. Hawthorn, the tree in our two stories, was the symbol of fertility and marriage. Its subtle, sweet scent and creamy-white blossom signified spring, a season of joyous celebration. The sacredness of the hawthorn was one reason why misfortune was believed to visit those who destroyed it, and clearly this tradition survives even to the present day.

The world of the ancient Celts and earlier settlers was one in which people were much closer to nature than we are. They considered the earth to be a living, breathing thing. While we have become detached from the natural world, from both its dangers and its beauty, our ancestors were much more in tune with the weather, the changing seasons, wild creatures and the innate rhythms of life. And they had to be, for their own survival. In doing so, they opened themselves up to another world – the world of the imagination, in which trees became imbued with sacredness. The druids, the priests or wise men of ancient times, believed trees to be sources of sacred wisdom. To them, sacred trees were no longer just trees: they became the embodiment of spirit.

THE SACRED YEW

Druids never built temples; they believed that nature itself was a temple. When Christians first came to these islands they often modified or destroyed the sacred groves. Sometimes a church would be built on a former pagan site, thus conserving its sacred powers and energies while also converting it to Christianity. The presence of yews in or near churchyards may be evidence of a pre-Christian tradition. There is a belief that some yews still growing in Britain and Ireland may predate the arrival of the first Christian missionaries.

Because the yew was sacred, it was considered unlucky to cut down or damage it, and only fallen trees were used. In her *Tree Wisdom*, Jacqueline Paterson describes the yew as one of the five magical trees of Ireland. The yew was most powerful in midwinter, symbolising the passage of the sun through the darkest time of the year. It was the tree of light, and its evergreen leaves emphasised the fact that life would continue. Yews were adorned with sparkling objects at Yuletide, to attract the light of the sun back into the year. The tradition continues even now with our Christmas trees. The druids made their magic wands and staffs from yew, and these could be used to powerful effect. The Children of Lir were each given a touch of a magic wand by their step-mother, when they were changed into four swans and condemned to remain as such for 900 years until the sound of a Christian bell released them from the spell.

THE MAGICAL HAZEL

In Celtic lore, hazel was the tree of knowledge. It had magical qualities; hazel twigs have been used since time immemorial for dowsing, or finding water underground. The hazel was central to one of the great legends of Irish folklore. Nine hazel trees grew around a sacred pool at the source of the Boyne River. The trees dropped nuts into the water and they were eaten by salmon, which thereby absorbed the nuts' wisdom. Druids revered the salmon and the number of bright spots on a salmon was said to show how many nuts it had eaten. One special fish swallowed all these magical nuts. A druid master, Finéagas, hoping to become all-knowing, caught the salmon and instructed his pupil to cook the fish but not to eat any of it. However, while the fish was cooking,

hot juice spattered onto the apprentice's thumb, which he instinctively thrust into his mouth to cool, thereby absorbing the wisdom of the salmon. The apprentice was Fionn Mac Cumhaill, who later became leader of the Fianna and a wise and mighty warrior.

THE TREE LAWS OF ANCIENT IRELAND

In Brehon law, as in our modern Forestry Act, there were sanctions for felling trees, but the ancient law was more complex. It divided trees into four classes according to their usefulness and symbolism, and there was a special fine for damaging each class of tree.

The most important trees were the 'chieftains': oak, with its acorns and phallic symbolism; hazel, with its branches that formed magician's wands; holly, with its red berries symbolising the food of the gods; yew, associated with death and rebirth; ash, symbolising health; pine, with its phallic-shaped cones; and apple, whose juice provided the drink of the gods.

The 'peasant' trees were alder; willow; hawthorn, associated with spring fertility rites; rowan; birch, symbolising the coming of spring and summer; and elm, associated with fairies or 'the little people' and the passage from life to death.

The 'shrub' trees were blackthorn, which heralds spring and guards autumn; elder, which provides bounty and health; aspen, symbolising the wind; juniper, offering purification; and reed, which was considered a tree because of its usefulness. The 'bramble' trees were dog-rose, bramble, fern and spindle, among others.

Opposite: A hazel rod traditionally used in water divining. Overleaf: A standing stone, carved with Ogham script; each letter represents a native tree.

Oak, one of the chieftain trees, was highly prized, not just for its tough, durable timber but also because its bark was used for tanning leather. Brehon law laid down that the penalty for stripping as much bark from another person's oak tree as would tan a cow hide was a pair of women's shoes worth half a *screpall*, and for as much as would tan an ox hide, a pair of men's shoes worth a *screpall*.

The law underpinned the utilitarian value of trees and the importance of their wise use with their spiritual and mythological values, reflecting the thinking and superstitions of the time. For example, in a story about the life of St Columcille, there was an oak tree in Kells that was greatly revered because the saint at one time had lived under it. One day it was blown down by a storm. 'And a certain man,' says the narrative, 'took some of its bark to tan his shoes.' But when he put on the shoes, 'he was smitten with leprosy from sole to crown,' in punishment for its desecration.

The ancient pagan myths and beliefs were carried over into Christianity, as if the new religion recognised a deep need to maintain the relationship we have had with trees since the dawn of time. Both trees and people are part of nature; even though we can choose to disconnect ourselves, as we have done in the recent past, we are ultimately inseparable from the great cycle of the natural world.

John Feehan, in his essay *The Spirit of Trees*, asserts that our relationship with trees is deeply rooted in our spiritual and psychological make-up. He believes this is why the presence of even a few trees or a grove or a wood makes us feel more at home, because we have been not only physically shaped by the ancestral landscape of our forest home, but psychologically and spiritually shaped by it also. Many other cultures share this experience.

For instance, throughout India, sacred groves can be found where the trees are strictly protected. Visitors to the sub-continent are astonished at how such a rich and colourful variety of wildlife still exists among such a dense human population. The reason is partly because of the widespread tradition of landscape and species conservation. All of the trees of a particular species, such as figs, might be protected as spiritual ancestors, and patches of forest are protected on behalf of local gods, stars and planets, and as symbols of the natural elements – energy, water, land and air. These sacred conservation practices are now being taken seriously by scientists because of their importance in biological conservation.

The primal link with trees and nature is also strong in Japan, which we tend to think of as a modern, technologically-led society. In Shinto, the dominant religion, almost every natural object, including forests and individual trees, can be inhabited by a spirit or god. Amazingly, two-thirds of Japan is still covered by native forests, and this is mainly because of the Shinto belief that they are sacred.

In Ireland, the rich tradition of veneration for nature has atrophied. We can see the consequences all around us, and it may be one of the reasons why we have had such a poor record in nature conservation. Having discarded our reverence for the natural world, we have had to rely on conservation laws, which the authorities attempt to enforce, as substitutes for that respect which our society should have retained.

Now, when a native wood or other nature site is threatened, only arguments relating to narrow scientific grounds are expected in defence. Feelings of love and respect for nature are regarded as irrelevant and, perhaps, even dangerous. And yet these are

among the most basic emotions that motivate us as human beings. When we take a walk in our favourite wood, we lean against familiar trees that have become old friends, we linger in sunny glades and dream, we watch wild creatures and tune our emotions to the rhythms of life. The woods speak to us in many ways, if we choose to listen.

For many of us, there is an unspoken reverence for nature's mystique, which is waiting for some catalyst, some turning point, to allow it to express itself. All over Ireland, people are becoming more conscious of their surroundings and their relationship with the natural world. This is reflected in the emergence of the many local groups set up to protect nature sites when they are threatened. Because of the contribution they make to our sense of place, our heritage and our imagination, native woods are attracting the greatest interest of all.

Overleaf: An ash tree in the eary morning mist

4 Individual Native Trees

Even as a background, trees persist
in being beautiful at every season,
their branches and birdsong an
indelible part of our sense of place,
our quality of life.

Alder

Irish *Fearnóg*
Latin *Alnus glutinosa*

*alder leaves
& berries*

ABOUT THE TREE On a trip down a canal or by a river, the tree most likely to be seen with its 'feet in the water' is the alder. Like the willow, the tree it is most commonly seen with, the roots of the alder provide a natural barrier to erosion, helping to stop earthen banks from washing away.

Alder grows quickly and can reach a height of 20 metres. It colonises new ground well, and is tolerant of a variety of conditions. Alder has root nodules that fix nitrogen, and so it can thrive on infertile soils. On more fertile soils, it is a productive forest tree.

Ballyfarnan, County Roscommon, means 'Mouth of the Ford of the Alder' (*Béal Átha Fearnáin*), while Ferns, County Wexford, comes from *Fearna* ('Alder Trees').

ABOUT THE WOOD Because it is resistant to decay under water, alder is used for making sluice gates for canals and piles. It is very suitable for turnery and for making furniture, and it was known as 'Irish mahogany' because of its reddish-brown colour.

20M

OM

Ash

Irish *Fuinseog*
Latin *Fraxinus excelsior*

*ash leaves
& seeds*

ABOUT THE TREE Ash is probably the most common native tree growing on farmland and in hedgerows. It is also one of the most widely planted hardwoods in Ireland. Ash is the last to come into leaf in spring, and the first to lose its leaves in autumn. The seeds – called 'keys' because they resemble medieval keys – are carried by the wind. Ash seeds itself very easily in hedgerows, abandoned gardens and roadside verges.

Ash trees can grow up to 45 metres high, but they do not live as long as oak. They can survive for about 200 years. They are quite shallow-rooting and demanding of soils, as many farmers will testify. Ash is not normally found on peaty soils. It also needs lots of light if it is to grow well.

ABOUT THE WOOD The wood is pale, cream-coloured, strong and flexible. The timber is very versatile and is used to make hurleys, oars, paddles, rudders, snooker cues, veneer for furniture, and window frames. The wood was even strong enough to make aircraft wings during the Second World War. Ash wood burns well, even when 'green'.

40M

0M

Aspen

Irish *Crann creathach*
Latin *Populus tremula*

ABOUT THE TREE Aspen belongs to the poplars, a family of quick-growing deciduous trees that grow in rich soils along the margins of rivers and lakes. It is not a common tree in Ireland but is widespread elsewhere in the Northern Hemisphere.

The leaves make a distinctive rustling sound and appear to quiver in the wind. The Latin name *tremula* means that the tree can often be heard before it is seen. The Irish word *creathach* in its name means 'shakey'.

The aspen can colonise new ground rapidly. As well as reproducing by means of seeds, it can also 'sucker', rather like the English elm. There is a danger, when planting aspen, that it may sucker too readily, and become invasive.

The aspen was the staple food of the beaver in Scotland before the animal became extinct in medieval times. Aspen shoots and leaves are popular with grazing animals, and aspen leaves were used as forage for livestock when grazing was scarce.

Glencree in County Wicklow is from the Irish *Gleann Crithigh*, meaning 'Valley of the Aspen'.

ABOUT THE WOOD Aspen produces a light-coloured wood that in other countries has been used for making matches, clogs, floorboards and pulp. When dried, the wood is very buoyant and, in the past, it was used to make paddles and oars. The Greek name for aspen is *aspis*, which means 'shield', and the ancient Celts did use the wood for that purpose.

aspen leaves

20m

0m

Birch

Irish *Beith gheal, Beith chlúmhach*
Latin *Betula pendula, Betula pubescens*

birch leaves

ABOUT THE TREE There are two species of birch in Ireland, and they look quite similar. Silver birch (*Betula pendula*) has a blackish, fissured trunk, while the downy birch's trunk (*Betula pubescens*) is usually smooth and whitish, and its twigs are softly hairy (hence the name 'downy'). Birches are small, short-lived trees and they grow to a maximum of 25 metres.

Birches are often seen on the margins of bogs, lakes and rivers. They can tolerate higher altitudes and poorer soils than other native species, and are very good at colonising disturbed ground. Birch is useful as a 'nurse' species that helps other forest trees to grow and as a soil improver. The leaf litter nourishes the soil and prepares it for other forest trees such as oak and pine, which, if left to nature, generally replace it over time.

Beith, the Irish word for birch, is found in quite a few placenames. For example, Ballybay, County Monaghan, derives from *Béal Átha Beithe* ('Mouth of the Ford of the Birch'). Glenbeigh, County Kerry, comes from *Gleann Beithe* ('Valley of the Birch').

ABOUT THE WOOD The wood is whitish, flexible and easily worked, and of average length. However, it rots very quickly when exposed to wet conditions. Its most common commercial use is for plywood and pulpwood. 'Birch bark' wine is made by distilling the sap. Leather was once tanned and made waterproof by treating it with birch 'tar'. In ancient times, people cut birch trunks for use as a walkway, or *tóchar*, over bogs.

20M

OM

*bird cherry
leaf & berries*

Bird Cherry

Irish *Donnroisc*
Latin *Prunus padus*

ABOUT THE TREE The bird cherry is so called because only birds can eat the cherries. Bird cherry is a smaller tree than its close relative, the wild cherry, reaching only 15 metres. Its distribution in Ireland is different, too. It is found mainly in the North-West, around Lough Gartan and Churchill in County Donegal.

The white flowers are borne on long stalks, unlike the wild cherry's, which are borne in clusters. The cherries are smaller and shiny black, rather than dark red, when ripe. Bird cherries like good soil and a sheltered site.

ABOUT THE WOOD The wood of both cherry species is the most valuable broadleaf timber grown in Ireland. It is in demand for turnery, furniture, veneers, and decorative panelling. It makes good firewood with a fragrant scent.

15M

0M

Crab Apple

Irish *Crann fia-úll*
Latin *Malus sylvestris*

ABOUT THE TREE Although crab apples can be seen mostly in hedgerows and around old farmsteads, the tree is a native of old oak woodland. Like cherry, it tends to be a species of the woodland edge, and it never dominates a wood in the same way as the major forest trees.

Crab apples are small, thorny deciduous trees that reach a height of 16 metres. The name derives from the Norse word *skrab*, which means 'scrubby'. Like wild cherry and rowan, crab apple makes a good ornamental tree in gardens and parks because of its attractive pinkish-white blossom and the apples which ripen in late autumn.

Anyone who has tried to eat crab apples will know how bitter they taste. They are used to make jellies, jams and wine. Many of the eating and cooking apples we enjoy today were cultivated from the wild crab apple, but without the thorns of the native tree.

ABOUT THE WOOD Crab apple wood is reddish-brown, hard and finely grained, and is used for carving and inlay work. It makes excellent firewood, giving a pleasant scent.

crab apple leaves

16M

0M

Hazel

Irish *Coll*
Latin *Corylus avellana*

hazel leaf

ABOUT THE TREE Hazel is a small deciduous tree or shrub that reaches a height of six metres. It is often found as hazel scrub, such as in the Burren. It is also found in association with ash or in the understorey of old oak woods. It has a lifespan of approximately 80 years, but coppicing can double the life of the tree.

The nuts are a good source of protein and are eaten by squirrels, mice and some bird species. Hazel was and still is cultivated for its nuts, although perhaps no longer in Ireland. Filberts are the cultivated form of the nut and are used in cooking and confectionery.

ABOUT THE WOOD Hazel is tough and flexible. Coppiced trees grow long, straight stems or sticks, which had many varied uses, including hoops for barrels, baskets, walking sticks, hurdles and thatching. The skill of coppice management of hazel, for basket-making, fencing panels and gates, is slowly being lost. Hazel sticks are used as rods for water-divining, adding to its already well-known mythical qualities.

6M

0M

Holly

Irish *Cuileann*
Latin *Ilex aquifolium*

ABOUT THE TREE Holly is a small evergreen tree that grows to a height of 15 metres. In many old native woods, holly can often be seen growing underneath the taller forest trees, forming what is called the understorey. Holly is a hardy tree and can be found on higher, exposed ground, where the wind contorts it into weird and wonderful shapes.

The trees are either male or female. Only the female bears the poisonous red berries which are so widely used for Christmas decorations. Demand is such that in some counties, such as Kerry, female trees are in danger of becoming extinct.

ABOUT THE WOOD The wood is dense and creamy-white with an even grain, used for carving, inlay and engraving.

holly leaves & berries

15M

0M

Sessile Oak

Irish *Dair ghaelach*
Latin *Quercus petraea*

sessile oak leaves & acorn

Oak is the largest and, together with yew, the longest-living native tree in Ireland. There are two species in Ireland, distinguished mainly by their acorns: the sessile oak has acorns with no stalks, while the pedunculate oak has acorns with long stalks. Oak has great symbolic significance all over Europe, not only for its fine, strong timber but also because it can grow to a great age and great size. Oak has been the subject of myth and religion for thousands of years. Most of our important native woods are oak woods.

ABOUT THE TREE Sessile oak is the more common of our two oaks, and it can be found on less fertile, acidic soils. For example, the western oakwoods of Killarney and Glenveagh are composed of sessile oaks. Old native oak woods can be very rich in plant and animal species.

Oak grows slowly as a seedling but at a faster pace as it matures, which is up to 200 years. Oaks can reach a height of 40 metres and can live for 1,000 years or more.

ABOUT THE WOOD Sessile oak is the more common forest tree, and it is cultivated throughout Europe for its fine timber. In the past, many of our best oaks were felled to make ships for Britain's Royal Navy, and oak was often used for structures such as roof beams. The roof of Drimnagh Castle in Dublin was restored using Irish oak beams.

The best quality oaks are used in the making of veneers. Oak is used for sawn timber, building timber, poles, fencing, firewood and charcoal. In the past, oaks in Killarney were used for smelting ore from the local mines. Tannin, used for tanning leather, used to be produced from oak bark. Oaks such as those in the Glen O' the Downs, County Wicklow, were coppiced.

40M

0M

Pedunculate Oak

Irish *Dair ghallda*
Latin *Quercus robur*

*pedunculate
oak leaves
& acorn*

ABOUT THE TREE
Pedunculate oak is usually found growing on heavy, lowland soils where it can also tolerate flooding. In most respects, the pedunculate oak is very similar to the sessile oak in terms of conservation value and timber use. It is less frequently used as a commercial timber tree. This species of oak grows in Charleville, County Offaly, and Abbeyleix, County Laois. The great King Oak of Charleville is a pedunculate oak. 'Derry' is a common element in Irish placenames, and is the anglicised word for *dair* (oak) or *doire* (oak grove). The name Dara also derives from the oak.

40M

OM

Rowan

Irish *Caorthann*
Latin *Sorbus aucuparia*

ABOUT THE TREE Also called mountain ash, rowan is a tough coloniser which can tolerate peaty soils and exposed conditions. It grows vigorously and reaches a height of 15 metres but it is not long-lived and lasts for up to 100 years. Like birch and ash, it needs plenty of light to thrive. Rowan is popular in suburban gardens because it is small and attractive in spring and autumn.

The familiar scarlet berries ripen by late summer and are a favourite food of thrushes and other seed-eating birds during the autumn and winter. The birds help to disperse the seeds. The berries can be cooked to make rowan jelly, which was traditionally eaten with game.

Drumkeeran, County Leitrim, derives from *Droim Caorthainn* ('Ridge of the Rowan').

ABOUT THE WOOD Rowan produces dense, pale-brown wood that can be used for turnery and carving. It was once widely used to make tool handles and, like yew, for making long bows.

rowan leaves & berries

15M

0M

*scots pine
needles &
pine cone*

Scots Pine

Irish *Péine Albanach*
Latin *Pinus sylvestris*

ABOUT THE TREE Scots pine was once abundant in the ancient wildwoods, especially on high ground and on less fertile soils. Ancient pine stumps exposed by peat cutting and erosion may be many thousands of years old. Most of the Scots pines seen now were planted from seed originally imported from Scotland, where native pine forest still survives.

Scots pine is a large evergreen conifer growing to a height of 40 metres. It can live for 300 years, but more typically 150 years. It is distinctive because of the bright orange bark in its topmost branches. It prefers light, sandy soils, and does not like sea winds or high rainfall. However, it can tolerate such conditions, and can be planted on marginal land where some broadleaf species could not grow initially. Thus it has an important role as a 'nurse' species for broadleaf trees.

The tree is a favourite with red squirrels, which prefer conifer woods, mainly because pine seeds are more palatable to them than the seeds of deciduous trees. Scots pine forests are, therefore, important habitats for red squirrels.

ABOUT THE WOOD Scots pine produces 'red deal', a strong, general-purpose timber. It is still used for fencing, joinery, building, flooring and telephone poles. Formerly, it was used for railway sleepers. The wood is slow to decay because of its high resin content. Sadly, it is now out of favour with Irish foresters because it is very slow growing and has been surpassed in volume production by tree species from western North America.

40M

0M

Strawberry Tree

Irish *Caithne*
Latin *Arbutus unedo*

*arbutus
leaves &
berries*

ABOUT THE TREE The strawberry tree, so named because its fruits look like strawberries, is not related to the strawberry fruit but to heather. It is a small, shrub-like evergreen broadleaf with leaves that resemble laurel. It is thought to be native to Ireland and not to Britain, but it is widespread in Spain and Portugal. It may have travelled to Ireland via a land-bridge from France or its seeds may have been carried by birds.

It is found mainly in Killarney, where it forms a large part of the natural forest on the islands and shores of the lakes. It is also found in Glengarriff Wood, County Cork, and around Lough Gill, County Sligo. Rocky outcrops and developing woodland are favourite habitats.

The strawberry-like berries are edible but have an unpleasant flavour although birds like them and spread the seeds.

ABOUT THE WOOD The wood of the strawberry tree is pink, fine-grained and very hard. There are no recorded traditional uses for it.

15M

0M

*whitebeam
leaves &
berries*

Whitebeam

Irish *Fionncholl*
Latin *Sorbus* species

ABOUT THE TREE

Whitebeam, like its near relative, the rowan, can be seen often in gardens and housing estates, where its ornamental qualities can be appreciated. It is a medium-sized tree and grows to 20 metres. Unlike rowan, it is unusual to see it growing in the wild and it is in evidence mostly in the south, where it prefers limey soils. The flowers are white clumps while the leaves turn gold before leaf fall. The red berries, which ripen in autumn, are attractive to birds. Like rowan, the berries are edible and can be made into jam and wine. Jelly made from the berries was traditionally eaten with venison.

ABOUT THE WOOD

Whitebeam produces a brown, hard wood, which is used in turnery, small furniture (such as the legs of stools), plywood and tool handles. The wood was also used to make cogs for some early machinery.

20M

0M

Wild Cherry

Irish *Crann silíní fiáin*
Latin *Prunus avium*

wild cherry leaf

ABOUT THE TREE Wild cherries, like crab apples, are usually found on the edges of woods and in old hedges, where their white blossom decorates the countryside in early spring. The trees grow quite quickly, reaching about 18 metres in height, and they live for about 200 years. They prefer fertile, alkaline soils, so will be seen more often in the East and Midlands. The cherries ripen by late July and August, and are quickly eaten by birds. They are smaller than the cultivated cherries and can be eaten, although they are mostly used for making syrups and cough mixtures.

18M

OM

Willow

Irish *Saileach*
Latin *Salix* species

*willow
leaves*

ABOUT THE TREE Willows are the quintessential waterside trees. There are many different species and they are sometimes difficult to distinguish. Willows grow rapidly and can be propagated easily from cuttings. Apart from the goat willow, most willows have long, narrow leaves. Some of the willows in gardens and parks are not native, e.g. the white willow, a tallish tree with a deeply fissured bark, and the weeping willow, which comes originally from China. The osier, used for basket-making, was introduced from Europe. The goat willow (also called pussy willow) has golden, male catkins, which are used in flower arrangements. The bark contains salicylic acid, from which the drug aspirin originated.

The name 'willow' comes from the Anglo-Saxon word *welig*, meaning pliancy, because the twigs and branches are so flexible. In continental Europe and parts of England, there is an old tradition of pollarding willows. The trees are cut above the first main branches, leaving thick stumps. It looks like the tree has been butchered, but new shoots spring from the stumps in spring and the tree quickly recovers.

This actually helps to rejuvenate the tree, which would otherwise rot much earlier. Willows are often used to stabilise canal and river banks, and they are more efficient than some artificial engineering works.

ABOUT THE WOOD Willow timber is usually very soft, and so is not as versatile as other hardwoods. It has been used for charcoal and fencing and, of course, basket-making. The Dutch use willow to make clogs.

25M

0M

Wych Elm

Irish *Leamhán sléibhe*
Latin *Ulmus glabra*

ABOUT THE TREE Up to about 5,000 years ago, elm was a dominant forest tree in the Irish lowlands, along with oak. Sadly, mature elms have been virtually wiped out by disease in recent years, and younger generations will only know what a mature elm looks like from photographs. Occasionally, one can still see young elms growing in old woods. Once the disease has run its course, elms may be free to grow into great forest trees once more. Wych elms are large deciduous trees that reach a height of 40 metres and can live for up to 500 years.

ABOUT THE WOOD Elm is a strong, supple, pale brown, heavy wood. It does not split easily and so was used traditionally for specialised purposes, such as water pipes, coffins, chests, wheel hubs and furniture. The wood from trees that have died from Dutch elm disease is prized by turners and sculptors for its decorative qualities. Like alder, the wood does not decay under water.

wych elm leaves & blossoms

40M

0M

yew
foliage

Yew

Irish *Iúr*
Latin *Taxus baccata*

ABOUT THE TREE Yews can live for an incredibly long time. Some trees in Ireland are estimated to be over 1,000 years old while specimens in Britain have been found over 5,000 years old. Although it is a native tree, it is most often seen in gardens, avenues and churchyards. The best place to see native yew trees is in Reenadinna Wood in Killarney National Park. This is Ireland's only native yew wood.

Yew is an evergreen conifer that grows to 20 metres. Older trees often divide into several distinct trunks. The red berries enclose a single seed and the needle-shaped leaves are poisonous to livestock, except deer. Yews prefer well-drained and sheltered sites.

Placenames called after yew include Terenure, Dublin, from *Tír an Iúir* meaning 'Territory of the Yew', Ballynure, County Antrim, from *Baile an Iúir*, meaning 'Homestead of the Yew'.

ABOUT THE WOOD The wood is reddish when freshly cut, turning brown. It is very durable and is used for furniture, tool handles, cabinet making, veneer and turnery. In the Middle Ages in Britain, yew was used for making long bows because of its strength and flexibility. Yew is probably the most valuable timber growing in Ireland at present and is much sought-after for high-quality furniture and craftwork.

Overleaf: Yew foliage and berries

20M

0M

5 Using Native Wood

As people have become more aware of the
beauty and heritage of trees and forests, they
have developed a desire for wooden objects in
their daily surroundings. We have to fulfil this
need in a sustainable way that does not harm
our forests or the functioning of the earth's
ecosystems. People with skill and vision are
needed to create beautiful objects in wood.

Those of us who love trees often find ourselves in a dilemma. We love trees because they are majestic beings. They live far longer than we do, they give us shelter from the wind and the rain, they dress a naked landscape, and their apparent permanence gives us a frame of reference with which to view the world. And yet, wood is one of the most beautiful, versatile and practical of raw materials. In order to produce wood, trees have to be cut down.

We only need to look around us with fresh eyes to see how important wood is to us. Wood has an impact upon us every day of our lives. The pages of books are made from wood. Wood is the universal environment-friendly commodity and is used in practically every facet of our lives: packaging, hygiene, shelter, heating, learning, communication and, of course, cradles and coffins. We like to walk on smooth, sanded maple floors, sit on chairs made from elm and alder, admire wooden furniture and dine from oak and beech tables. While most new houses in Ireland are made from brick and concrete, wood is used for roof beams, stairs, doors, floors, skirting boards and architraves. It is increasingly being used in house frames. Wood is also used to make composites such as medium density fibreboard (MDF), oriented strand board, hardboard and chipboard.

So many products are made from wood that we sometimes forget it has to come from trees. And these trees have to be cut down and fashioned into the familiar objects that surround us. In the Western world, most trees end up in sawmills or pulp mills. Ireland currently imports 500 million euro worth of timber products, two-thirds of which is paper. Ireland's imports of tropical wood in 2000 reached 120 million euro and we are the largest per capita importer of tropical wood in Europe. This means that other countries have to produce the wood that we demand. Ireland's ecological footprint extends far beyond our shores, to Europe, Africa, Asia and the Americas.

Much of our quality broadleaf resources have long since been cut down. Even after the depredations of the nineteenth century, the exploitation of broadleaf woods continued, particularly during the First and Second World Wars, when southern Ireland was economically isolated. Some of our woods were simply too young to be cut down in the early part of the twentieth century, and that was the main reason why they survived at all. Because the Government in the Republic concentrated on building up the softwood industry since Independence, broadleaf woods were neglected. It became a vicious circle. There was little good-quality timber, so woodland owners could not ensure a continuous supply, and so the hardwood industry could not develop.

The argument against growing hardwoods is simple, say Ireland's commercial timber growers: hardwoods are uneconomic, they demand a lot of hard work, and it takes a longer time to produce a decent crop. It's much easier to grow conifers, they say, and there's a market for them.

It is not surprising, therefore, that much of the wood we use is imported. Maple, oak and pine come from the United States, beech from France and Germany, iroko, teak and mahogany from West Africa and elsewhere. Even some ash for hurleys has come from Wales. Ireland consumes large amounts of hardwood, especially tropical hardwoods. The great forest trees crash to the ground in the Ivory Coast and Ghana to supply Irish

Overleaf: Michael Quirke working on carvings made from native Irish timber in a former butcher's shop in Sligo

pubs, hotels, homes and furniture makers, leaving behind a devastated landscape. Ireland is the fifth largest furniture manufacturer in Europe, according to Jan Alexander, an Australian, founder of the tree conservation organisation Crann and a tireless promoter of homegrown hardwoods and of forestry practices that are gentler to nature.

Irish people are largely unaware that, by buying wood from forests that are not sustainably managed, they are eating into the world's priceless reservoirs of biodiversity.

'Hardwoods are a lot of bother,' Jan Alexander says, 'but we live on a wonderful planet, which is worth bothering about.' She also makes the more immediate point that continental European countries for the most part grow their own hardwood timber profitably, and then sell it to us! But the continental Europeans have the advantage that they never lost their native forests or their forestry traditions, so they have an existing resource to draw on. If we are to produce more hardwoods, even native wood, for the home market and take pressure off natural tropical forests – and we should – we will have to start virtually from scratch.

WORKING WITH WOODS NATURALLY

How long will it take to develop a viable hardwood industry, where native timber is used for the familiar products that surround us? When will we be able to walk into shops and see furniture and kitchen units in native oak, or floorboards made from home-grown birch?

Joe Gowran, of Muintir na Coille (Coppice Association of Ireland) has been working with native woods for most of his career, operating from his base in County Sligo. He believes in managing woods in ways that are as close to nature as possible. 'Working against nature can be counter-productive,' he argues.

'If one tries to imitate the existing woodland or what is likely to have grown there in the first place, one should have healthier trees and therefore greater productivity in the long term.'

The aim of this type of forest practice is to maintain the woodland as an ecosystem, rather than over-exploit it. Joe Gowran does not under-estimate the size of the task ahead. 'It could take 30 years for some woods to produce reasonable timber of sawlog quality,' he says.

SUSTAINABLE USE OF WOODLANDS

While many native woods should, and will, remain strict nature reserves, other native and non-native woodlands can be restored and managed in order to produce a new and valuable wood resource. This will mean active management that involves cutting down some of the trees to allow for the development of trees of better-quality wood. It may not be easy for people to get used to the concept of felling trees as an essential pathway to native hardwoods of better quality. The noise of the chainsaw has become for some synonymous with destruction. However, wood is a very important commodity, and plantations produce wood to meet the demands of the market. We like hardwood floors, pine kitchen units, oak beams, ash window frames and ornamental tables, and bowls made from yew and cherry. It is better to grow the hardwoods we require in plantations than to over-exploit native woodlands.

If we are to have these things, we must develop new approaches to using woodlands. Wise use in this context means the optimum

Opposite: Hurley ash ready for finishing

sustainable use of the resource without damaging the ecosystem. This means working with nature rather than against it. The new guiding principle is 'sustainability'. The idea is that sustainable use must not only be compatible with nature but also must not exclude economic and social well-being. Ireland has signed up to international agreements that commit us to sustainable use of our forest resources. This promises to be a real challenge to us.

CERTIFICATION OF WOOD PRODUCTS

The environmental movement has been campaigning for many years to protect the world's native forests and to produce wood from plantations in a sustainable way. Wood product suppliers have felt the impact of this campaign and they, in turn, have put pressure on the forest industry to ensure that wood and non-wood products are produced from forests that are sustainably managed, whether these are native woods or plantations. Out of this, a system of certification of wood products has been developed.

The idea behind certification is that consumers have a choice of buying products that are certified as coming from verifiably sustainable sources. A label is attached stating the source and the fact that the goods and/or services have been produced from sustainably managed forests. Forestry companies who sign up to a code of practice associated with certification undertake to ensure that the natural environment is not abused. Different certification systems operate now in many wood-producing countries but all have a common focus. Wood producers who choose

Opposite: Craftsmen in Letterfrack Furniture College using native timber on a restoration project for the National Museum

not to be included may in time lose their market share.

In principle, certification of wood products should be a good incentive to make forestry gentler to nature, and it has already had a few positive effects. But will it revolutionise the way we treat our forestry resources in Ireland? It would seem that it will take more than certification to achieve the vision that Irish conservationists want. The problem is that the conditions to which the forestry industry signs up may not be sufficiently strong to ensure substantial change. Meanwhile, consumers may be convinced that a label on a wood product means what it says, but the reality could be different.

We have the makings of a classic tussle between the idealists and the pragmatists. The idealists want to see Irish forestry based on native broadleaves which are managed in a way that is as close to nature as possible. The pragmatists say that this is unrealistic because we need to supply much larger volumes of wood, especially softwood, than that which such broadleaved woods could supply, and the forest industry is strongly based around quick-growing, non-native conifers like Sitka spruce. The pragmatists, who are often involved in the forestry industry, believe that Ireland has moved some distance towards meeting environmentalists' demands. There are very generous grants for planting and maintaining broadleaves, and the eventual aim is to increase the annual planting of broadleaves to 30 per cent of total annual planting. Irish forest policy, as implemented by the Forest Service of the Department of the Marine and Natural Resources, is now based on the principles of sustainable forestry management (SFM), and broadleaf trees form a cornerstone of this policy.

There are many measures in place to promote broadleaf trees at all stages of the

'forest cycle', from seed to timber and beyond. The National Broadleaf Breeding Programme and ongoing research into the use of native birch are aimed at promoting the quality and vigour of the trees from the word 'go' when it comes to creating new broadleaf woodlands. The Forest Service is also funding organisations such as Woodlands of Ireland, the Tree Council of Ireland, Crann, and Conservation Volunteers Ireland (CVI) in their efforts to raise public awareness of, and involvement in, broadleaf trees and woodlands. All of these initiatives are designed to encourage the development of a broadleaf culture and an appreciation of the beauty and value of our native trees. Should all these things encourage us? Possibly. The problem remains that broadleaf trees are still not popular among commercial timber growers, so environmentalists see the government's measures as slow and tentative. We will explore this subject further in the following chapters.

In Northern Ireland, although the amount of semi-natural native woodland that remains is less than 10,000 hectares, there is considerable activity aimed at conserving it and increasing the cover of native woodland. Remnants of upland oak are scattered around the country. The best-known oak woods are those at Rostrevor on the northern shores of Carlingford Lough and Breen in north Antrim. Upland mixed ash is the natural woodland on base rich soils and is most common in Fermanagh and Antrim. Wet woodland, where alder and willow predominate, are scattered throughout Northern Ireland, with good examples on

Opposite: A native hardwood floor – now a much sought after product
Above: A rustic coffee table made by Eltjo van der Laan

the fringes of Lough Neagh and the Erne basin. Wet woodland dominated by birch is colonising much cutaway and degraded bog.

The UK Biodiversity Strategy lists these three types of woodland as priority habitats and Habitat Action Plans have been published for each of them. These plans include targets for both restoration and expansion. The Woodland Trust is about to embark on an inventory of ancient woodland that will provide useful baseline data. The Forest Service is developing strategies to meet the targets. It has already made the decision to restore to native woodland about a quarter of its ancient woodland sites that carry plantations at present.

As people have become more aware of the beauty and heritage of trees and forests, they have developed a desire for wooden objects in their daily surroundings. We have to fulfil this need in a sustainable way that does not harm our forests or the functioning of the earth's ecosystems. People with skill and vision are needed to create beautiful objects in wood. In the past 20 years, a new wave of artists and craftspeople has emerged in Ireland, aided by bodies such as the Crafts Council. Training opportunities have burgeoned in the third-

level colleges and through the establishment of Letterfrack Furniture College, with funding from the Forest Service. From such institutions, a new generation of artists in wood has emerged.

Many pioneers and innovators, from Ireland and elsewhere, have set up wood-based businesses in the past 30 years. Their skill with wood has helped draw other people to their vision. Often their use of wood has been part of a deeper philosophy of the need to live in harmony with the world around us. The craftspeople that feature in this chapter are typical of many of these innovative and creative people.

ELTJO VAN DER LAAN, DUTCH FURNITURE MAKER

Eltjo van der Laan started his own wood-working business in north Groningen in Holland at the age of 20. As far as Eltjo is concerned, Ireland is in many ways the exact opposite of Holland. 'A crooked tree in Holland would be cut down, whereas I like the imperfections in Irish wood, and I work with them,' he said. His hand-made rustic furniture may display some of nature's

imperfections, but it is beautifully made and finished.

Eltjo lives and works in Ballinamore, County Leitrim, close to the recently restored Shannon-Erne waterway. He has restored Lawderdale House and the old courtyard is now the centre of his business, where he has installed a showroom, workshop and sawmill, with an air-drying shed in the old walled garden.

Although he likes to work with all types of wood, he loves working with Irish native timber, and he sources most of his timber from within a radius of 70 kilometres. 'I probably have the most fun with Irish yew,' he says. 'It has a fantastic texture and colour, but it is extremely dense and splits very easily.

'I made 20 oak coffee tables three foot wide from one tree I bought for 190 euro, and this was worth 8,253 euro when made into furniture.' The business is concentrating on making those coffee tables, chairs and big dining-room tables. His main market is Ireland, with about a quarter of his output going to the UK and other parts of Europe.

Eltjo also grows his own trees on 135 hectares, a mixture of broadleaves and conifers, including Scots pine.

HAND-MADE KITCHENS

Why would someone use Irish native wood when so many good woods are available from overseas? Áine O'Callaghan, who designs custom-built kitchen units with Tim O'Sullivan, in Glanmire, County Cork, responds: 'There is no comparison between Irish and North American hardwood. Irish

Above: Eltjo van der Laan takes a piece of native timber to create a coffee table.
Opposite: Eltjo's air-drying facility. Drying is vital for top-quality products.

wood is beautiful and far more interesting. Every time you work a piece of Irish wood it's completely different to that which went before.'

There is such a great variation in Irish wood that each kitchen they make is individual and distinct. They started the business 10 years ago, specialising in hand-made, high-quality, low-production products.

THE 'DUNBRODY' REPLICA EMIGRANT SAILING SHIP

The severe shortage of Irish timber in the nineteenth century was the main reason why the *Dunbrody* sailing ship was built in Québec in 1845. It was one of eight ships of similar size operated by the Graves family, based in New Ross, County Wexford, who traded in Europe and the Americas. Part of their trade was in emigrants. The *Dunbrody* was beached off Labrador in 1873 with no loss of life, and that was the last that was heard of it, until over 100 years later.

In 1991, the John F. Kennedy Trust, based in New Ross, began the work of building a replica emigrant ship to the same design as the original *Dunbrody*, but this time using as much Irish timber as possible. The idea was to create a major tourist attraction based on the maritime heritage of New Ross. It was the brainchild of local entrepreneur Seán Reidy, and was further developed by Garrett Fallon.

'We found the original bill of sale in the

Opposite: Below deck in the Dunbrody, *a replica famine ship in New Ross. The ship is made from home-grown timber, unlike the original which was made in Québec! Previous: Detail of the* Dunbrody *deck. Overleaf: Sculptor Michael Casey works on a 'Madonna and Child' made from bog wood in his County Longford studio.*

Graves' family papers and this gave us precise dimensions and descriptions of the ship,' says Seán Reidy, who manages the *Dunbrody* project. 'There are eight-inch thick Irish oak frames, with larch planking below the water line and Douglas fir above, with the masts and spars in the same wood. The average length of planking was 40 foot, averaging five foot thick and steamed to shape. We now have a ship that has been made with great attention to detail and is fully seaworthy.'

Coillte supplied some of the timber for the ship, which was built in the old Ross boatyard.

SCULPTURE IN BOG WOOD

Oak, yew and pine stumps, which are thousands of years old, are the raw materials for Michael Casey's remarkable bog wood sculptures. He returned to Ireland in 1960 and works with his son, Kevin, in his workshop in Barley Harbour, Newtowncashel, County Longford. At first he worked as a carpenter, but then, one day in 1970, he saw his first piece of bog oak.

It took a long time for him to see the potential of this wood for the craftsman, longer still to see its potential on the plane of art. But bog oak, bog yew and bog pine are all woods and Michael Casey's long and dedicated apprenticeship had by now made him a true master of woodcraft. He knew much of what he saw in that piece of bog oak, recognised it for what it was and was confident in how to handle it. He discovered how to make it dry and still sweet, he learned to polish it and make it glow, dark and alive, and he began to shape it.

6 The People's Millennium Forests

Native trees are important because they have evolved with other plants and animals that are adapted to life on this island and they provide the most ideal woodland ecosystems. It is no accident that native woods throughout the world have the most value for wildlife, especially if they are allowed to grow naturally without too much human interference.

Why are our native woods special? The uniqueness of the Irish is a myth borne out of our long cultural and geographical isolation. We have been enriched by many different cultures over the centuries, and our so-called pure Celtic blood has been well diluted by now. Could we say the same about Irish nature? Should we treat it as separate and unique, or should we celebrate other, non-native plants and animals, which could add to our existing wildlife diversity?

Native trees are important because they have evolved with other plants and animals that are adapted to life on this island and they provide the most ideal woodland ecosystems. It is no accident that native woods throughout the world have the most value for wildlife, especially if they are allowed to grow naturally without too much human interference.

Non-native trees will continue to be planted, and their beauty and usefulness are part of nature's grand design. However, we need to reclaim much more space for native woodlands, for their own intrinsic value and to provide a home for a range of plants and animals that find difficulty living elsewhere.

IN CELEBRATION OF NATIVE WOODLAND

Most of the woodlands we see around us have been established as commercial plantations. Native woodlands are very different, however.

In a native woodland, there is an eclectic mix of young, mature and old trees of different species and in different shapes and sizes. Trees that are allowed to die naturally decay on the woodland floor, replenishing the soil as they do so with vital nutrients so that new life can begin once more. In a native woodland, seeds germinate where they will, instead of being planted. There is neither artificial fertilisation nor pruning, nor large-scale felling. Trees that are misshapen or that do not grow vigorously would be taken out of a commercial plantation, whereas the 'imperfections' in a native wood are part of its character, diversity and wonder.

The way that native woods are allowed to evolve has a significant influence on their natural value. Older and more extensive woodlands have had more opportunity to grow as nature intended and, if protected from domestic animals, are usually richer, with their associated heritage of wildlife.

We might compare a woodland to a town, which starts out as a cluster of houses but which, as it grows, begins to develop its own identity. If the town is centuries old, it may have wonderful old buildings and monuments that have become places to treasure. It will have lots of interesting people and many different places in which to live and work. This combination of old and new and the variety of experiences shape the town and it develops what we might call 'character'. The same is true for a native wood. It has many places for animals and plants to live in, and, just like a town, it is home to a diverse community. Wildlife communities in native woodlands can be very rich and interesting, and many of the world's animal and plant species are found in such woodlands.

In a woodland, the trees, and the animals and plants they support, are dependent on one another. Their root systems are intertwined in a vast network in the soil that nourishes and supports them. The soil itself is like a living organism, a hive of activity and home to a myriad of life forms. Some of these we can see, like earthworms, ants and beetles;

Previous: A young tree-hugger
Opposite: Children learning more about woodlands on a school nature trip

many more we cannot see, like bacteria and fungi. They help to aerate and fertilise the soil or make vital nutrients available to plants. The roots of the trees reach deep into the earth and tap into water supplies and nutrients, which are brought up through the trunks and into the leaves and branches, helping the trees to grow.

Old trees, leaves and twigs fall to the ground and the soil animals and micro-organisms begin the composting process, breaking them down so that the nutrients they release can be taken up again by the roots. When old trees die they make space for saplings, which shoot upwards towards the light to claim their place, and so on in an endless cycle of growth, decay and re-birth.

The trees themselves depend on one another for support and shelter. Trees such as holly and hazel can grow in the shade underneath the canopy of larger forest trees, e.g. oak, while birch and ash like plenty of light. Cherry, crab apple and hawthorn prefer the sunnier woodland margins. Light is very important in woodland. A diversity of insect life, such as butterflies, can be found in sunny glades. The top layer, or canopy, is the engine that drives the woodland ecosystem. The leaves capture sunlight and make food with carbon dioxide, water and sunlight. A whole community of creatures make their homes there, including moths, whose caterpillars feed on the leaves.

In the same way that people become more interesting as they grow older, trees also develop an identity, richness and dignity as they mature. Their fissured bark and the scars of broken branches offer homes to countless tiny animals, and their boughs become bedecked with ferns, mosses and lichens.

Bird life in native woods is often very diverse because the insect or other animal life on which the birds feed is itself plentiful and diverse. The treecreeper, with its long, hooked beak, knows how to prise beetle larvae from underneath the bark, while tits and barn owls use small holes as nests. The jay, a shy bird of deciduous woodland, eats and stores acorns, but the ones that it forgets have the chance to germinate and grow into mature trees. This is one way that oak woods can spread. The woodcock seeks the shelter of the woodland floor for nesting and roosting. Sparrowhawks dart in between the trees hunting for small birds. Buzzards ride the air currents around woodland, expecting to find mice, rabbits or carrion. And these are just a few examples of the types of birds one can see in native woodlands.

Although some of these species can be found also in broadleaf plantations, these are not ideal habitats for wildlife because they simply cannot offer the diversity of places for them to nest, roost and feed. Scientific studies have shown consistently that many more animals and plants can exist in native woodland than in broadleaf plantations. An entire book could be written about the wildlife in our woodlands, but we can only provide a few snapshots here. The bibliography will guide you towards more detailed sources of information.

One might ask, if nature was so good at growing our original native woods, why do we need to intervene now? Why do we not just leave them alone and let them grow? Part of the answer is that non-native species, which were introduced in the last few centuries, can be more aggressive and can take over from native species. Laurel and rhododendron, ornamental shrubs beloved of Victorian gardeners, stifle the growth of tree seedlings and smother the wild flora that is special to old woodland. These shrubs must be removed and kept under control if the woodland ecosystem is to flourish. In the early years of Irish forestry, non-native conifers were often planted in state-owned native woods. Since the 1990s, Coillte, the Irish Forestry Board, and Dúchas The Heritage Service have been removing them.

The other main problem is grazing and browsing. Cattle, deer and wild pigs were part of Ireland's woodland ecology for thousands of years, but their domestic descendants do not perform the same function. Large grazing animals are an integral part of natural forests around the world. We have lost the predators of grazing animals, such as wolves, that kept the numbers of grazers in check. If the grazing pressure is too high, harm can occur to the natural process of regeneration. Even though deer are much loved by the public, red deer, which is believed to be the only native species still extant, can do considerable damage to the woodland. Introduced species such as fallow and Sika deer have multiplied out of control, eating seedlings and stripping the bark from young trees. For this reason, deer fencing and regular deer culling are necessary.

Similarly, rhododendron and cherry laurel, both invasive exotic species, have infested many of our native woodlands, creating deep shade that suppresses natural ground flora and natural regeneration. As with deer, managing these species will be key to efforts aimed at reinstating our native woodland cover.

NATIVE WOODS FOR THE MILLENNIUM

The originators of the People's Millennium Forests Project were aware that creating or restoring broadleaf woods was not enough. Many of the broadleaf trees that have been planted since the 1990s are non-native and in plantations. The People's Millennium Forests Project embraces woodland restoration, education and awareness raising, wildlife conservation, and training in woodland management. All these ingredients are essential if we wish to bring our most important natural habitat to centre stage.

The two main aims of the People's Millennium Forests Project are to make the public more aware of native woods and to restore a variety of native woodlands around the country. Sixteen woodland sites are being restored, and a tree has been planted for every household in the country. This involves planting around 1.2 million new trees from native seeds, many of them gathered by voluntary organisations, schoolchildren and local community groups.

In choosing the woodlands to be restored, it was important to have a good spread of woodland types, to reflect the natural diversity of native woodland throughout the island. Because nature does not recognise political boundaries, the Forest Service Northern Ireland is involved in restoring two woods (Favour Royal and Castle Archdale) in the border areas. (A list of the Millennium Project woodlands is provided in the Appendix.)

The People's Millennium Forests Project began in 1997, when the Woodlands of Ireland Committee was established. It included representatives of all who were concerned with and interested in native woodlands. Some 5.1 million euro has been allocated to the project, with 2.5 million euro provided by the sponsors, AIB, and the remainder by the National Millennium Committee, the Forest Service and Coillte, the Irish Forestry Board.

Overleaf: Foliage and berries from yew trees lying on the forest floor. Leaves from the yew are poisonous to livestock but birds feed on the fruit.

The People's Millennium Forests Project is being managed by Coillte, the Irish Forestry Board. Coillte holds a substantial amount of native woodland on behalf of the people of Ireland.

John McLoughlin, Chief Environmental Officer with Coillte, explains its role: 'Our aim is to restore and expand the native woodlands in our care. We will manage them in a sustainable way, using low-impact forestry practices to extract timber, which will be processed through our sawmill in Dundrum, County Tipperary. The problem is that the woods are mainly even-aged, a legacy of the exploitation between the First and Second World Wars. We want to bring back more "naturalness" by creating woods with young, mature and old trees. This uneven structure is much better for wildlife. We will be felling small areas and allowing these areas to fill in with young trees and other vegetation before proceeding with the next, and so on.'

People can see Coillte's work in the People's Millennium Forests Project at 12 of its woods spread throughout the country, one site owned by Westmeath County Council at Portlick, County Westmeath and at the Yew Wood in Muckross owned by Dúchas. With the help of funding from the sponsors AIB, the National Millennium Committee and the Forest Service, conifers, rhododendron and laurel are being removed, deer fencing erected and many new native trees planted.

Michael Doyle is in charge of the restoration of 5,000 hectares of native woods managed by Coillte. He explains that if a native wood has been neglected for many years, the first task is to remove the non-native trees which will often include conifers like spruce, and broadleaf trees like beech and sycamore. Any logs of reasonable quality will be sold as commercial timber and the rest sold as firewood. Invasive laurel and rhododendron will also be removed. The first 'cut' will create clearings that will be either planted with young native trees, or the wood allowed to regenerate naturally. When clearings are made, trees tend to colonise the spaces without human intervention if there is a good seed source close by. On some sites where commercial conifer plantations have been felled, birch colonises rapidly. Where, previously, foresters would clear the birch for the next crop of conifers, in some forests a new native birch wood will be allowed to grow, often without any assistance.

Should we be encouraged by what is being done for our native woodlands? The answer is yes, because something positive and exciting is happening after years of neglect and inactivity. Real people are working on real projects on the ground instead of just talking about them. Native seeds are being collected by local groups and schools and grown in nurseries. Invasive shrubs and non-native trees are being removed, and native trees are being planted. These small beginnings should give us encouragement for the huge task of reforestation that lies ahead. We shall explore the future in more detail in Chapter 7.

7 A Vision for a New Millennium

Native forests are valuable genetic storehouses where a myriad of plants and animals with their own specific genetic pattern make up what is called genetic biodiversity. Native forests throughout the world have evolved over thousands of years and, in the case of the tropics, over millions of years. Their value for the conservation of genetic diversity is incalculable. Every year, biologists discover new species of plants and animals, among the millions already discovered. Tragically, species are also lost each year when native forests are destroyed in quest of timber or for farming.

It is a glorious day in early June as we walk up the steep, rutted track through the mossy oaks of Killarney. The leaves still have that fresh, light-green colour of spring, and shafts of sunlight dance on the woodland floor beneath. We emerge from the leafy canopy out into open country, still climbing upwards, with Mangerton mountain sweeping up to our left. Only some scrawny, wind-whipped holly bushes interrupt the desert-like expanse of heather and bog. Several red deer graze, well camouflaged but alert, in the middle distance.

Some distance up the hill, in the shelter of a rocky outcrop, is a deer-fenced hectare that Rory Harrington has brought me to see. Rory is an ecologist working with Dúchas The Heritage Service. He has made an experiment to see if native woodland can be introduced once more to the bare uplands. Although it is easy to grow trees in most places, here on exposed heath and bog it is more of a challenge.

Rory points to a soil profile he dug to illustrate the problems. 'When the trees were removed, rain leached minerals from the top layer of soil and they accumulated in this grey layer below. The roots cannot penetrate the difficult horizon to reach the rich, brown earth underneath. We have to break up this layer so that the trees can establish themselves properly and thrive.' Evidently, deforestation brings about ecological changes that are awkward to reverse.

Oak, birch, Scots pine and holly are now flourishing here, and the stronger-growing pines are providing valuable shelter for the young broadleaf trees. Looking beyond the little plot to a far valley, small tongues of scrubby woodland cling tenaciously to the steep hillsides, showing that native woodland can survive here, given half a chance. This is just one example of the work going on behind the scenes to restore and re-create our native woodlands.

Previous generations believed that the development of civilisation had to go hand in hand with the retreat of the forests. First it was agriculture. Then it was industrial development, followed by housing and roads, all of which needed land. And so, the forests yielded up their treasures in the cause of progress. But, as civilisation progressed, we discovered that natural forests often have hidden values we learn to cherish and cannot do without. The great rainforests that girdle the equator and the boreal forests of northern Europe, Russia and Canada are essential for climate regulation. Our own forests are contributing to this process albeit in a smaller way. Forests are the earth's lungs, inhaling huge amounts of carbon dioxide from the atmosphere, converting it into plant matter, and exhaling oxygen. The Earth itself works like an organism, and the breathing in and out of the forests is as vital for the planet as it is for us as individuals. Indeed, oxygen is one of the great forest products, rarely appreciated or recognised.

Native forests are valuable genetic storehouses where a myriad of plants and animals with their own specific genetic pattern make up what is called genetic biodiversity. Native forests throughout the world have evolved over thousands of years and, in the case of the tropics, over millions of years. Their value for the conservation of genetic diversity is incalculable. Every year,

Opposite: A soil profile dug into the hills above Killarney, showing the grey, impoverished layer a few centimetres below the surface. This layer discourages root penetration and has to be broken up so that trees can establish themselves properly and thrive.

biologists discover new species of plants and animals, among the millions already discovered. Tragically, species are also lost each year when native forests are destroyed in quest of timber or for farming.

All over the world, popular movements have been formed to protect the remaining native forests, now that we know how valuable they are. In the United States, 95 per cent of the original forests were felled during the last few hundred years, and bitter battles have been fought between the authorities and logging companies to save the last old growth stands in Washington and Oregon. People have literally risked their lives to save redwoods that were standing before Columbus arrived. Across the border in British Columbia, Canadians are trying to save ancient stands of Sitka spruce and Douglas fir, some of the tallest trees in the world. In Scandinavia, huge areas of ancient forest have been logged and replaced with plantations; in thickly forested Sweden, only one per cent of the original, untouched primeval forest survives.

CONSERVATION OF IRISH NATIVE WOODS

In Ireland, the conservation movement is younger than those of most of our neighbours. Since the island was virtually stripped of trees a century ago, we lost our tree culture and, with it, our reverence for trees and for wild nature. The native woods that survived the clearances were not valued because of their poor timber quality and because priority was given to agriculture. Since Independence in 1922, foresters concentrated on growing plantations just for timber, first with a mix of broadleaf trees and conifers and then, after the Second World War, mostly with conifers. In an unsuccessful effort to add value to native woods, many

were underplanted with conifers, a practice that ceased in the 1970s.

The first native wood to receive official protection was in Killarney, when the Bourne Vincent family donated its estate, with its famous oak woods, to the nation in 1932. Almost 50 years passed before any more would be protected officially. In the 1970s, the movement to conserve woodland and promote tree planting was led by An Taisce, the Irish National Trust. It provided the foundation for the emerging tree culture we see now.

In the 1980s, Jan Alexander founded a new organisation with a focus on broadleaf forestry, called Crann. Over a period of about 25 years, Crann and other voluntary groups such as the Tree Council of Ireland have campaigned persistently with few funds and little public understanding to give broadleaf and native woodlands the attention and care they deserve. These efforts are now beginning to bear fruit.

Resulting from the Wildlife Act of 1976, the State responded to the need to conserve ancient native woods when, in 1980, they were among the first to be included in a new international network of nature reserves. Now, there are about 6,000 hectares of woods in nature reserves and national parks in Ireland. This is still tiny by European standards, and many woods without state protection are vulnerable to development and neglect. There are possibly another 40,000 hectares in need of full protection. Many are still not documented or mapped and are not always in sympathetic ownership.

Every year, a small amount of native woodland is lost to development; when it is added up over the decades, this gradual attrition is significant. 'Ancient woods are easily our most decimated habitat,' says Jim Lawlor, one of the founders of the Native

Woodland Trust, the first organisation dedicated exclusively to the cause. 'Our view is that we should lose not as much as another square yard. Even if we manage to save every single native wood left in the country, we will still have less than the area of protected bogs.'

The aim of the Trust is to acquire a number of ancient woods, and to promote community ownership to give us a renewed feeling of responsibility towards them. Ultimately, the Trust believes that private or community ownership is the best way to keep and manage native woods.

Concerned individuals and small groups have played a crucial role in saving a number of native woods from destruction or in drawing public attention to their plight. Tomnafinnogue Wood (see Chapter 2) was saved from the chainsaws by the actions of a few determined people. In the late 1970s, the last part of the great forest of Coolattin began to be felled. Two local people, Johnny Couchman and Paddy O'Toole, kick-started the campaign to save the woods. Local politicians and government ministers initially were not interested and tree legislation was ineffective.

The felling continued unabated through the early 1980s. A turning point was reached when the then Opposition Leader, Charles Haughey, was quoted as saying: 'I have seen a video of the destruction. If I am elected, I will take a very personal interest and will do whatever I can to save it.'

Paddy O'Toole, a local farmer and publican, was involved in the secret removal of tree tags from the wood at night. He organised about 25 people, including local farmers, accountants and teachers from Dublin to do this. Under legislation, the tags had been placed on the trees that were due to be felled. Once removed, the trees could not be felled until another survey had been

carried out, crucially delaying the felling.

At the same time, a high-profile campaign was led by Thomas Pakenham, author of *Meetings with Remarkable Trees* and himself a woodland owner. That campaign succeeded in raising funds, which were then matched by the Government, to buy the wood and secure it for posterity.

In the early 1990s, an ancient wood called Ballyseedy, a few miles from Tralee, County Kerry, was threatened by a new dual carriageway, even though 80 per cent of it was owned by Kerry County Council. Ballyseedy is all that remains of the forest that centuries ago extended over much of the Dingle peninsula and up to Listowel. The wood was designated a Special Area of Conservation under EU law. It is a natural ash/alder river woodland that, like The Gearagh, is virtually extinct in Europe. One of the alders, over 30 metres high, is believed to be the tallest in the Republic. A campaign mounted by local people and An Taisce succeeded in persuading the European Commission not to fund the new road through the wood, and it is now considered reasonably safe, at least for the moment.

At the start of the Millennium Year, Offaly County Council announced that its preferred route for the Tullamore by-pass was through part of Charleville Wood, on the outskirts of the town. This ancient wood has some of the most impressive oaks in Ireland and, like Ballyseedy, is designated as a Special Area of Conservation. On this occasion, Dúchas ensured that a major survey of the wood was carried out. At the same time, a number of concerned local people began a campaign to raise awareness about the wood and they commissioned their own survey.

The end result of all this work was that Dúchas decided to double the area of woodland and other habitats designated for

protection. Offaly County Council has now recognised that it cannot cut through the wood and it has accepted that an alternative route will have to be found.

In the 1990s, the existing road through the Glen O' the Downs in County Wicklow was scheduled to be upgraded to a dual carriageway. In the process a narrow strip of woodland would be removed from both sides of the existing road. This sparked off a high-profile campaign to save the woodland planned for removal. Glen O' the Downs had been one of the first nature reserves to be created. A number of idealistic young people took to the trees and refused to come down until the trees were spared. Although the local press and Wicklow County Council were unsympathetic, some of the national media coverage presented them as the 'Eco Warriors'. The campaigners continued for two years, surviving bitter winter weather and extreme discomfort, before finally agreeing to conform to a High Court order to vacate the woodlands or face imprisonment.

A few individuals who are prepared to stand up and be counted often make changes in the status quo. Jan Alexander is one. She wanted to re-forest the country with broadleaf trees. A simple vision, clearly articulated, and the courage to declare it were needed. In a very different way, the 'Eco Warriors', in spite of their failure at the last hurdle, succeeded in making it more difficult for officialdom to dismiss the case for woodland conservation in the future.

Freda Rountree was another inspirational person, closely associated with Crann for many years, and appointed Chair of The Heritage Council by the then Minister for Arts, Culture and the Gaeltacht, Michael D. Higgins, in the mid-1990s. Among her many

Opposite: A nesting box

initiatives was the idea of a nation-wide project on native woodlands to coincide with the Millennium. People like Jan Alexander and others in Crann, The Tree Council and the Society of Irish Foresters adopted the idea with enthusiasm, when they came together in 1997 and established Woodlands of Ireland. The proposal for what became the People's Millennium Forests Project (see Chapter 6) was submitted to the National Millennium Committee, a body set up by the Government to identify ways of marking the new millennium. That the sponsors, AIB, and the Forest Service of the Department of the Marine and Natural Resources, finally approved the project with such enthusiasm vindicated the vision of many and the persistence of a few. Sadly, Freda Rountree died before she could witness the success of the initiative she had inspired.

THE NATIVE WOODLAND SCHEME

Perhaps one of the biggest advances in the reinstatement of Ireland's native woodlands, and a clear example of an enlightened approach to nature in the twenty-first century, is the Forest Service Native Woodland Scheme. The scheme, developed by the Forest Service in partnership with Woodlands of Ireland, Dúchas The Heritage Service, Coillte, Regional Fisheries Boards and others, offers support to landowners to conserve existing native woodland and develop new areas of native woodland. Its overall aim is to encourage the proactive protection and expansion of Ireland's native woodland resource and associated biodiversity, using appropriate 'close-to-nature' management.

The scheme is based on solid ecological principles that reflect the core biodiversity objectives involved. For example, each project must include the development of a detailed long-term management plan based on an ecological survey; site disturbance is to be kept to a minimum; the use of natural regeneration is encouraged; existing habitats of value are to be retained. Projects are also required to promote the most appropriate native woodland type for particular parts of the country, in an effort to reinstate the rich mosaic of native woodland habitats that once covered the countryside.

Much has changed in the past decade in respect of official policy towards supporting such a scheme. Until recently, grants were directed mainly at the establishment of commercial forests. The new scheme is targeted on 15,000 hectares of existing native woodland and it aims to create another 15,000 hectares of new woodland. In total, this is roughly equivalent to the combined area of the Wicklow and Glenveagh National Parks.

For this grant scheme and other conservation measures to operate fully, a new appreciation of the aesthetic and environmental value of native woodlands is required. It is the totality of the woodland with all its components from soil micro-organisms to canopy tip, and the relationships between them, that constitute the woodland. We need to find again our lost sense of respect and reverence for our trees and woods. Nature writer Michael Viney expresses it well when he says: 'I would like to see a new relationship between people and trees – or rather, an old one brought up to date. When local communities depended on trees for timber, large and small, they learned to respect them as living things, to extend their lives and productivity through coppicing

Overleaf: 'Growing your own'; oak seedlings on a windowsill

and pollarding, and felling in a way that kept the whole wood healthy and regenerating.'

The Forest Service Native Woodland Scheme will help to revive traditional ways of managing woodland. Coppicing, for example, is an age-old practice where the tree is cut near the base of the trunk and allowed to re-grow. Many stems will emerge from the one stump, which are useful for a variety of products. Another practice, seen mainly in some countries in continental Europe, is that of maintaining continuous forest cover, where single or small numbers of trees are felled. This is in contrast to the usual practice of clear-felling crops of similar age. Apart from the dramatic aesthetic impact upon the landscape, the environmental benefit of continuous forest cover is considered to be greater than clear-felling.

The prospect of establishing substantial areas of new native woodlands under the scheme is a challenge to landowners and foresters alike. Many of these woodlands will be beside existing woodlands or along waterways. Extending existing small woodlands improves both the scale and diversity of the expanded woodland, adding to its ecological value. In addition, planting along rivers to create riparian woodland helps to re-establish a scarce habitat. Trees are also excellent at absorbing excess fertilisers that are otherwise flushed off from intensively-farmed land to pollute waterways.

Creating habitats that act as wildlife corridors and stepping-stones is an additional benefit of the scheme. Often referred to as 'ecological connectivity', these act like a series of interconnected routes through which animals and plants can travel. Such habitats are an added benefit in situations where the planning authorities may have overlooked the ecological benefits of maintaining woodlands as components of the countryside.

A VISION FOR THE NEW MILLENNIUM

There has never been as much hope for the future of Ireland's native woodlands as there is now. Several voluntary organisations, local communities and local authorities are dedicated to promoting their particular conservation goals through their own individual innovative schemes. State support for reviving and expanding native woodlands throughout the country through the People's Millennium Forests Project and the Native Woodland Scheme is a testament to the interest that exists in the protection of our indigenous natural heritage. Local communities are beginning to flex their muscles to protect trees and woods under threat, with some success. People are more aware of trees than ever before. The re-forestation of Ireland is under way.

A new era in forest awareness and appreciation has begun that could see our landscape become softened and more benign. As in the past, when placenames, traditions and even alphabets were linked to trees and forests, so too can our new woodlands become core ingredients of a new culture in Ireland.

Ireland in the future could be a place of forested valleys and hills, and changing colours throughout the seasons, as is the case in France, Germany and Canada. Like these countries, it could be a place where native woods are embraced by its citizens as central to their culture.

We must not allow ourselves to come complacent, however. More needs to be done in advocating the need for care and maintenance of woodlands, in celebrating our personal enrichment through the medium of trees, in advancing awareness of the value and beauty of wood, and finally in fulfilling our debt to future generations for the omissions of the past. At present, greater emphasis is given to the expansion of commercial conifer plantations. A target of 15,000 hectares of new native woodland over five years may seem a lot, but this is roughly the same as the area of conifer plantations established every year, with substantial funding from the European Union and the Irish taxpayer. In 2001, the proportion of broadleaf plantation was 13 per cent of total annual planting.

Alongside the development of sustainably managed broadleaf plantations, there is still much more room for native woodlands to expand. Our barren, desolate hills could become wooded once more with native woodlands of Scots pine, birch and oak. And it should not be a case of 'broadleaf trees are good' and 'conifers are bad'. The cutaway boglands of many parts of Ireland reveal the bleached skeletons of trees that were buried beneath a protective blanket of peat for several thousand years. Most of these are Scots pine. This tree is the mainstay of the Caledonian forest, the very epitome of the Scottish central highlands, and a present-day representation of ancient Irish pine forests.

The example of Scotland should be Ireland's inspiration. Great efforts are being made there to restore and expand Scotland's ancient pinewoods. Since 1972, the Woodland Trust in Scotland has extended its care to 1,000 sites covering 17,500 hectares (equivalent to the total area of Ireland's nature reserves). The sites range from nationally and internationally important sites to small urban and village woods. Ancient woodlands account for 360 sites (6,200 hectares). The Trust has created 2,200 hectares of new native woodland and has a target of creating a total of 3,000 hectares by 2003. In the process, it is creating one of the largest native woods in Scotland.

The future is not set in stone. Pioneers and visionaries do not wait for history to unfold – they make it. What sort of vision would be consistent with the newly emerging tree culture started by idealists of 30 years ago?

There is no reason why we could not recreate the wildwood in our own hills. Coillte has already made a decision to use lower ground for its commercial plantations. The more remote hills could be converted gradually to native pine and birch woods, leaving the commercial plantations to the better land and relieving the overgrazed and ravaged uplands. On the more fertile lowlands, one can envisage a mosaic of broadleaf and conifer plantations, and native woodlands, some kept as strict nature reserves and others used for recreation, timber and wildlife. Oak, ash and alder woods would follow the river valleys and link with farms and nature reserves. Today, only one per cent of the country is covered by broadleaf woodland of all types. Ten per cent coverage with native woodlands would be a good initial target to aim for. This would not happen immediately but gradually, over decades.

Local communities would own more native woods. With ownership comes responsibility, and this is one way in which nature could be conserved more effectively in the long term.

Michael Viney strikes a chord when he remarks that: 'A local broadleaf wood brings character to any place, marking the seasons with a changing beauty. Children need woods especially, as a focus of magic and mystery – and as the best outdoor classroom.'

He goes on to say: 'We must also find room in Ireland for at least one sizeable broadleaf forest – big enough to get lost in – which is not planted for any kind of timber and in which nature alone holds sway. We owe this ecological sanctuary, sacred not only to trees, but to birds, badgers and beetles, as atonement for the past and revelation for the future.'

The face of Irish forestry could change beyond all recognition in the next 30 years. Change is already in the wind, but a better vision will not become a reality unless we, as citizens, listen to the visionaries and pioneers and support them. This generation of Irish people is the first to have the money, the know-how, the understanding and the imagination to make such a vision happen. A good start would be to create a native wood big enough to get lost in.

All the Millennium Project woodlands are state-owned. Twelve are in the care of Coillte, the Irish Forestry Board. Favour Royal and Castle Archdale are managed by the Forest Service Northern Ireland, Muckross is part of the Killarney National Park, managed by Dúchas The Heritage Service, and Portlick is owned by Westmeath County Council. All these woods are open to the public. Indeed, this is an essential part of the project, so that people can enjoy them and learn more about an important part of the island's natural heritage.

BALLYGANNON, COUNTY WICKLOW

Ballygannon Wood, situated one km from Rathdrum, is part of the Clara Vale Nature Reserve. The Irish name, *Baile na gCanónach*, means 'the Town of the Canons'. The canons, who had been brought to Dublin by St Laurence O'Toole in the twelfth century, owned land near Rathdrum. A large part of the woodland was cleared before 1750 and many more trees were cut down during the two World Wars. Now the woods are mainly oak, with holly, hazel and rowan. Interesting bird species include jay, long-eared owl, woodcock, wood warbler and crossbill.

CAMOLIN, COUNTY WEXFORD

Camolin Wood is about 10 km south-west of Gorey town. The name comes from a religious house founded by St Molin, second Bishop of Ferns, who died in the seventh century. The presence of Bronze Age burial sites dating from at least 1000 BC indicates a continuous human presence from that period, and no doubt the woods were used over the centuries for timber, fuel and food. Two unusual plants found there are cudweed and toad rush.

CASTLE ARCHDALE, COUNTY FERMANAGH

Castle Archdale is 20 km north-west of Enniskillen on the eastern shore of Lower Lough Erne. The name comes from a castle that was built in 1617 by John Archdale of Suffolk, who was granted extensive lands during the Ulster Plantations. The site itself has had no woodland for many centuries past, but it is surrounded by plantations. Castle Archdale is in the parish of Derryvullan. 'Derry' or *doire* in Irish means 'oak grove'. The woodland heritage is further confirmed by the nearby village of Lisnarrick, in Irish *Lios na nDaireog* meaning 'The Fort of the Little Oaks'. The aim here is to create a new native woodland with alder, ash, birch and oak, and to see how trees colonise some of the areas left unplanted.

COILL AN FHALTAIGH, COUNTY KILKENNY

This wood, the largest of the millennium forests, lies about four km from Kilkenny City. It was once part of the Brittas Estate, home of the O'Rourke family. The current Ordnance Survey maps refer to this site as 'Woodlands', the name of the townland where it is situated. However, in local tradition, this wood is known as Coill an Fhaltaigh or 'Wall's Wood'. Restoration of the wood includes planting with oak, ash, alder and birch. Some Scots pines have been retained to provide a habitat for the native red squirrel. Blackcap and spotted flycatcher are among the less common woodland birds found here.

CULLENTRA WOOD, COUNTY SLIGO

Cullentra, on the southern shores of Lough Gill, County Sligo, grows on a promontory overlooking the Lake Isle of Inisfree, made famous by Yeats's poem of that name.

'Cullentra', from the Irish *Cullentragh*, translates as 'A Place Producing Holly'. During the last century the area was described thus: 'The district was formerly a natural forest as is still the portion of it called Slish Wood, with its hardy oaks, all of mature planting rising from the water's edge and clothing the precipitous mountain side ...' The Down Survey of 1633 found considerable tracts of woodland in the area. The wood is the most northerly station of the rare strawberry tree, one of only three locations in Ireland where it is found growing naturally. Areas that were planted with spruce and pine have now been cleared and replanting with native trees is taking place.

DERRYGILL WOOD, COUNTY GALWAY

Derrygill Wood lies close to the village of Woodford and, together with nearby woodlands at Derrycrag, Rosturra and Pollnaknockaun, it is one of the last remaining fragments of what was once an extensive area of forest. Derrygill derives from 'Derry' or in Irish *doire*, an 'oak grove or wood' and *gall*, which means 'foreigner'. Derrygill therefore means 'Oakwood of the Foreigner'. The site has been extensively planted with commercial conifers and stands of Scots pine that were planted in the 1940s still remain. Some of these will be retained as part of the native species mix that is currently being planted. The pine marten, Ireland's rarest mammal, is found here.

DERRYGORRY, COUNTY MONAGHAN, AND FAVOUR ROYAL, COUNTY TYRONE

These two woods are essentially part of one forest because they lie beside one another on both sides of the border north of Monaghan town. Derrygorry probably means 'Oakwood of the Goats'. Favour Royal Demense derives its name from Favour Royal Bawn, a large fortified mansion house, the ruins of which still survive. Favour Royal Bawn was built by Sir Thomas Ridgeway in 1611 and so named because the land was granted as a royal favour from James I. Much of the area was planted in the 1940s with non-native conifers, which are being harvested at present. At both sites oak occurs with hazel, ash, birch, hawthorn, alder, blackthorn and willow. A large herd of fallow deer ranges across the estate but these will be excluded from the woodlands by a deer fence.

GLENGARRA, COUNTY TIPPERARY

Glengarra, in Irish *An Ghleann Garbh*, which means 'the Rough Glen' or 'Garra's Glen', is in the Galtee Mountains about 12 km west of Cahir. Oak trees cling to the sides of the Burncourt River valley. Alder and silver birch grow well close to the river and wet, boggy areas. At the base of the slopes, old ash trees dominate with hazel, holly, rowan, wych elm and grey willow. Scots pine grows up to 30 metres high in places. Forest floor plants include yellow pimpernel, bilberry and lady fern. Rhododendron invasion is a serious problem and is being eradicated, while alder, ash, birch and oak are being planted.

LACCA, COUNTY LAOIS

Lacca Wood is on the southern slopes of the Slieve Bloom mountains, about six km north-west of Mountrath. Translated from the Irish, Lacca has several meanings, including a 'Stone or Flagstone,' 'The Side of a Hill' and 'A Place Full of Stones or Flags'. Until very recently, the trees were mainly Norway spruce, beech, Scots pine, oak, grey willow and birch, with some rowan and holly in the

shrub layer. In time, the more natural ground flora in the vicinity will spread throughout the newly planted woodland. Alder, ash, birch, cherry and oak will be planted and natural regeneration encouraged.

MUCKROSS, COUNTY KERRY

The Muckross peninsula is part of the Killarney National Park, which contains the largest area of native woodland in Ireland. A large part of the peninsula is very special because it is dominated by one of the scarcest native trees in Ireland, the yew. The yew wood at Reenadinna is particularly rich in bird life, and includes the blackcap and wood warbler. A deer fence will be erected to prevent damage to young trees. Muckross means 'The Wood of the Pig' and this almost certainly refers to the use of the wood in ancient times as pasture for pigs. The peninsula is home to a host of native trees, shrubs, plants, mosses and lichens. They include hazel, oak, willow, birch, ash, aspen and the rare strawberry tree. The herb layer has sedges, yellow loosestrife, the marsh fern and wood millet, a plant found only in old native woodlands. There are also a number of rare orchids and a huge variety of lichens, liverworts and mosses.

PORTLICK, COUNTY WESTMEATH

Portlick is on the eastern shore of Lough Ree, eight km north of Athlone. Portlick, meaning 'Part of the Flagstone Surface', refers to the limestone bedrock that occurs extensively in the region. Portlick is a native hazel/ash woodland with lesser amounts of oak, whitebeam, holly, alder, willow, birch and hawthorn. The first Ordnance Survey maps (1837-1838) do not indicate forest here, which suggests that woodland has colonised the area from other nearby woodlands since 1900. The Dillon family occupied the estate for several centuries and built the medieval tower house, Portlick Castle, which is still occupied today. Apart from the removal of non-native trees such as sycamore and beech, hazel coppicing will also be carried out.

ROSSACROO-NA-LOO, COUNTY KERRY

Rossacroo-na-loo is an old oak woodland 10 km from Kilgarvan. Rossacroo derives from *Ros* meaning a 'wood or grove'. Historical evidence indicates that the area has probably been wooded for many centuries. At the northern end is a disused railway line, which operated from 1891 to 1959. The most common native tree is sessile oak, accompanied by downy birch and holly, rowan, hazel and alder in the shrub layer. The forest floor and the boughs of the trees are covered in a luxuriant carpet of mosses, lichens and ferns, which flourish in the moist Atlantic air. Among the less common wildlife found here are the barn owl and the horseshoe bat. Non-native trees and shrubs, especially rhododendron, are being removed and a deer fence erected.

ROSTURRA, COUNTY GALWAY

Rosturra is close to the village of Woodford. The name comes from *Ros* meaning 'wood', while the neighbouring townland of Derrylahan comes from *doire*, the Irish for an 'oak grove or wood'. Rosturra is very unusual because it contains yew mixed with oak, with some ash and birch. Other notable shrubs occasionally found include holly, hazel, willow, hawthorn, spindle-tree (*Euonymus europaeus*), buckthorn (*Rhamnus catharticus*), blackthorn and guelder rose. Among the more unusual wildlife are the

brimstone, silver-washed fritillary and ringlet butterflies. Non-native conifers have been felled in recent years and these will be replaced with sessile oak, alder, ash, birch and Scots pine.

SHELTON, COUNTY WICKLOW

Shelton, named after the abbey at Shelton close to Arklow, was formerly the seat of Lord Viscount Wicklow. Shelton is part of the Wicklow oakwoods, once the second largest oak forest in Ireland. An eighteenth-century traveller wrote that: 'the extent of the woods induced me to imagine I was in the midst of one of those immense forests seen only on the continent'. Today, that great woodland has been reduced to small fragments. Broadleaved woodland still dominates the area though there has been much planting of other non-native species, notably beech and conifers. The main aim in Shelton is to plant native trees such as oak, ash, alder, birch and hazel on a green-field site.

TOURMAKEADY, COUNTY MAYO

Most of the current forest site, on the western shore of Lough Mask, County Mayo, was densely wooded in the early nineteenth century. Bishop Plunkett planted the forest with oak, larch and Scots pine after the tenants had been evicted from his estate at that time. Native trees include oak, birch, rowan, alder, hazel, willow, holly and ash. There is also a considerable amount of conifers, which are currently being harvested, and beech, rhododendron and laurel, which will be controlled. Native trees will be planted in the clear-fell areas, including alder, ash, birch, oak and Scots pine, and fences will be erected to exclude the local herd of Sika deer.

CHAPTER 1

Mitchell, Frank, *The Shell Guide to Reading the Irish Landscape*, Michael Joseph/ Country House, 1986.

CHAPTER 2

Aalen, F.H.A., Ken Whelan and M. Stout, *Atlas of the Irish Rural Landscape*, Cork University Press, 1997.
Excursions of the Royal Scottish Arboricultural Society to Dublin, Powerscourt, Coollattin, Carton and Killarney: and also to Dolphington, Lanarkshire, Edinburgh, 1897.
McCracken, Eileen, *The Irish Woods since Tudor Times*, David and Charles, 1971.
Neeson, Eoin, *A History of Irish Forestry*, The Lilliput Press, 1991.
Quirke, Bill, *Killarney National Park – A Place to Treasure*, Collins Press, 2001.

CHAPTER 3

Feehan, John, 'The Spirit of Trees', *Millennium Supplement, Releafing Ireland*, Summer 2000, Crann, Banagher, County Offaly.
Joyce, P.W., *A Social History of Ireland*, M.H. Gill, 1971.
Paterson, Jacqueline M., *Tree Wisdom*, Thorsons, 1996.
Simon, Ben, 'Tree traditions and folklore from northeast Ireland', *Arboricultural Journal*, Vol. 24, AB Academic Publishers, 2000.

CHAPTER 4

An Introductory Guide to British Native Trees, British-Trees. Com: http://www.british-trees.com/guide
Flanagan, Deirdre and Laurence, *Irish Place Names*, Gill & Macmillan, 1994.
Lucey, Anne, 'Yuletide brings no cheer to the holly tree', *The Irish Times*, 12 December 2001.

Our Trees: A guide to growing Ireland's native trees in celebration of a new Millennium, The People's Millennium Forests Project, 2000.

CHAPTER 5

Joyce, Pádraic M., *Growing Broadleaves*, COFORD (National Council for Forest Research and Development), National University of Ireland, Belfield, Dublin 4, 1998.

CHAPTER 7

Growing for the Future: A Strategic Plan for the Development of the Forestry Sector in Ireland, Forest Service, Department of Agriculture, Food and Forestry, Stationery Office, Dublin, 1996.
Native Woodland Scheme, Explanatory Leaflet, Forest Service, Department of the Marine and Natural Resources, Leeson Lane, Dublin 2, 2001.
Peterken, George, *Natural Woodland: Ecology and Conservation in Northern Temperate Regions*, Cambridge University Press, 1996.
Seeing the Woods for the Trees: The Woodland Trust's Approach to Conservation, Woodland Trust, Autumn Park, Grantham, Lincolnshire, NG31 6LL, 1999.

WEBSITE ADDRESSES

Woodland Trust:
http://www.woodland-trust.org.uk/
Forest Service: www.marine.gov.ie
The People's Millennium Forests Project: www.millenniumforests.com
Coillte: www.coillte.ie
AIB: www.aib.ie